Baseball in Pittsburgh

*An Anthology of New, Unusual,
Challenging and Amazing Facts
About The Greatest Game
As Played in The Steel City*

Edited by Paul Adomites and Dennis DeValeria

*With exceptional help from Jack Carlson, Bob Carroll,
Frank Cunliffe, Jeanne DeValeria, Norman Macht, Sally O'Leary,
The Pittsburgh Pirates, and Denis Repp*

Cover design and illustration by Bud Boccone

Table of Contents

BASEBALL IN PITTSBURGH (ISBN 0-910137-61-7) is published by The Society for American Baseball Research, Inc., P.O. Box 93183, Cleveland, Ohio, 44101. Copyright 1995, The Society for American Baseball Research, Inc. All rights reserved. Reproduction in whole or in part without written permission is prohibited. Printed by Mathews Printing, Pittsburgh, PA.

An Interview with Art McKennan

By Ed Luteran and Jim Haller

Art McKennan began his association with the Pittsburgh Pirates as a 12-year-old boy in 1919. He worked many different jobs with the Bucs, from batboy to usher and scoreboard operator for the 1927 World Series, before he became the Forbes Field public address announcer in 1948, a job that brought him his greatest fame. When he retired early in 1993, he had spent more than 70 years in the national pastime.

This interview was conducted by SABR members Ed Luteran and Jim Haller shortly after McKennan announced his retirement. It was conducted for the Oral History Department of the Baseball Hall of Fame.

E&J: Tell us how you started with the Pirates back in 1919.

Art: My father began taking me to Forbes Field when I was nine years old in 1916. I loved baseball. I loved Forbes Field and its environment. I loved hearing the bats smack the ball during batting practice as we walked near the ball park. I loved hearing the program sellers pitching their wares as we entered the park. I loved the entire atmosphere of Forbes Field.

I loved it so much that the occasions my father took me weren't often enough. So, I decided to go over to the ball park and get a job. This was in the summer of 1919 after school was out. I took my lunch and simply sat by the players' gate waiting for some kind of miracle. On my first attempt, Billy Southworth came along and took me inside. He played right field at the time for the Pirates and later managed National League pennant winners in St. Louis and Boston. He took me inside the building, but not into the clubhouse. That was against the rules. Manager George

Gibson simply would not allow any kids into the clubhouse, for a lot of reasons. I used to sit on the trunks that the team used for traveling around the league. The trunks were located just outside the clubhouse. I would just sit and wait for odd jobs, any jobs. I'd wait for the clubhouse man to come out and give me something to do. After a while, he got very used to seeing me sitting on those trunks, day after day, thanks to Billy Southworth.

The clubhouse man started sending me on errands for the players. He sent me out for lunches. He sent me to the cleaners with dirty clothes and things that needed to be sewed. He made me a real handyman.

Forbes Field had a huge distance from home to the screen behind the plate. It was a little over 100 feet. The Pirates had a "foul tip" boy located at the screen to return foul balls to the umpire in order to save time. The "foul tip" boy was my second job and batboy was my third position with the Bucs.

I was the Pirate batboy for all of 1920

and 1921, and for part of the 1922 season. There was a point in 1921 when we were sure we were going to win the pennant. We were six or seven games ahead of the New York Giants in the latter part of August and feeling very confident. We went to New York, lost a five-game series and never recovered. I had experienced a great high and a great low in a matter of a few days.

In the middle of the 1922 season, one

I finally graduated from high school in 1925. I started working for a manufacturing chemist located across the street from Forbes Field. We could actually stand at our upstairs windows and look into Forbes Field and see the games.

But my position there got confused, so I returned to Forbes Field as an usher. In 1926 I started working for a stockbroker in down-

A dapper Art at the public address mike.

of the fellows operating the scoreboard left and I took his job. It was the "junior" job because two men operated the scoreboard. But it paid one dollar a game, which was more than the batboy position paid: just a couple balls per game. That's all. By the end of the 1921 season, I had a trunk full of balls. The kids in the neighborhood loved me. Shortly after I took the scoreboard job, the other operator left and I became the "senior" operator. Two dollars a game. I was still in high school and feeling very proud of myself.

town Pittsburgh, and at that point I was completely divorced from the ball club.

In 1927, a friend of mine was running the scoreboard in order to put himself through Pitt dental school. I decided to help him — without pay — during the World Series so that I could spend time on the field with the great Yankees.

No question, the Yankees were great, but they did not intimidate the Pirates as some people have contended. Our guys were professionals. The Yankees did not overwhelm them.

The Pirates had been world champions just two years earlier, and we were basically the same team. A few guys had left, but things were still similar. The Yankees had tremendous power and were very explosive, but somebody dreamed up all those intimidation stories because of the sweep.

I continued working in the scoreboard, helping my friend, for several seasons. In fact, I helped him, not only with the Pirates, but with the Homestead Grays and gained an excellent exposure to black baseball.

In September 1930, I was playing golf in Schenley Park when I noticed that my legs were getting very weak. I was having a very difficult time walking up the hills, and decided to play only nine holes that day. I went home early. Before 48 hours had passed, I could no longer move my legs, even when lying in bed. My Uncle Tom, a neurologist at St. Francis Hospital, was called in to look at me (my father had died in 1924), and he diagnosed polio. At one point some doctors thought I might have meningitis, but my uncle's diagnosis was right.

He placed me under the care of an orthopedic surgeon who turned me over to a young physiotherapist named Jesse Wright. She was working her way through Pitt as a physical therapist. Eventually, she became a renowned orthopedic surgeon. In fact, there is an annual medical award at Pitt in her honor. I am scheduled to present it next year, and I look forward to the moment. I was one of her first patients.

It took me 11 years to recover and get back on my feet. They got me into the swimming pool at the Pittsburgh Athletic Association, and I swam there for 56 years. I am certain that the swimming has given me the strength to get this far in good shape despite the polio.

E&J: How did you get back to the Pirates after the polio setback?

Art: I started going to the games in a wheelchair. I was sitting in a wheelchair along the right field line, in fact, on a Saturday afternoon in May, 1935, when Babe Ruth hit his final three home runs. He was very methodical that day. He hit the first homer in the lower deck. He smashed the second into the upper deck, and he clobbered the third over the right field roof.

E&J: How did the crowd react to the Babe's three blasts?

Art: There were some 12,000 to 13,000 people at Forbes Field that day. There was no great reaction in the crowd. There was no overwhelming astonishment. Of course now over 100,000 people have claimed they were there that day. The Babe was not highly overweight as they made him out to be in the recent movie, "The Babe." In fact, as I recall, he even had a single that day. But, after that day he traveled to a couple more cities with the Braves and then retired from the game.

E&J: What about your return to the Pirates in 1948 as the Forbes Field public address announcer?

Art: Well, I actually returned to the Pirates in 1942. A friend of mine started working with the Pirates at the time the Bucs installed the electric scoreboard, the public address system and the lighting standards. He was the first man to run the electric scoreboard from the press area up behind home plate. He got a regular job in 1942 that prevented him from doing the scoreboard at the same time. I was not working at the time, so he turned it over to me and I ran the scoreboard for the next 50 years.

E&J: Let's talk about the 1925 World Champs. This team is not well remembered by most people in Pittsburgh today. Who was its best player?

Art: Without question, its best player was Pie Traynor. I saw Brooks Robinson play, and he was an excellent third baseman, but he wasn't any better than Pie. A writer in Pie's day coined a phrase: "so-and-so doubled down the left field line, but Pie Traynor threw him out at first." He made all kinds of plays at third base, especially bare-handed grabs. He was an awkwardly built person, all shoulders and rather stooped. He was unusually tall. He generally resembled shortstop Glenn Wright. In fact, Traynor, Wright and Joe Cronin all played in the Pirate infield at one time, and

Former Pirate teammates, Traynor (R) and Charlie Grimm.

they all looked somewhat alike as far as size goes. For their day, they were all unusually tall. But to me, Pie Traynor was the finest third baseman I ever saw play. He was a true leader.

E&J: Tell us about the seventh game of the 1925 World Series.

Art: I was ushering at the time. I had the section that Mrs. Walter Johnson was sitting in. She was a nervous wreck. However, Washington jumped in front of the Pirates in the first inning, 4-0. It was raining from the beginning of the game. It was a very light rain, almost a spray. And, it was Johnson's third start of the Series. Game officials wanted to get this game in. It had been postponed the

day before. And as it turned out, the rains fell for quite a while after the last game. The weather turned absolutely sour, and they may not have played the seventh game for another week or so. But the umpires pushed on with Game 7 just to get it in. The Pirates won with a two-out, three-run rally in the eighth inning. It was almost as exciting as the last game of the 1960 World Series here in Pittsburgh.

Washington had some big hitters on that 1925 squad. They had Goose Goslin, Sam Rice, Bucky and Joe Harris, Roger Peckinpaugh and Ossie Bluege. Peckinpaugh was the American League most valuable player that year. However, the Pirates had a very good hitting team of their own that year with a team average over .300. They had four men with over 100 RBIs each.

George Grantham and Stuffy McInnis shared first base. Eddie Moore played second. Wright and Traynor covered the left side of the infield. Clyde Barnhart, Max Carey and Kiki Cuyler manned the pickets with Earl Smith and Johnny Gooch doing the catching.

McInnis had been around baseball forever. I believe he had been in the American League with Boston. Carey had been playing for the Pirates for an awfully long time as well. I think every Pirate starter except Moore hit .300. And, of course, Cuyler was the hero with the hit down the right field line that got entangled in the canvas and drove home the winning runs. An irony in all of this was Joe Harris, who played for Washington in the 1925 World Series, played for Pittsburgh in the 1927 World Series.

E&J: Tell us about the Waners.

Art: Paul came along in 1926. In fact, he asked permission to bring his kid brother to spring training. Of course, that was Lloyd, a second baseman at the time, who replaced Max Carey in center field. Both Waners were singles hitters. They were batting magicians. Paul was an excellent right fielder. He played that strange wall in right at Forbes like you and I eat lunch. In fact, during the early 1950s the Pirates brought Paul back to Pittsburgh to teach Gus Bell to play the wall, and Bell resented it for some reason. Bell's reaction greatly upset Manager Billy Meyer, and Bell did not stay long with the Bucs.

E&J: Did Waner ever transfer any of those right-field tricks to Clemente?

Art: No. Clemente was an absolute natural in everything he did in baseball. He picked up things on his own very quickly. He was a great self-teacher. He told me one time that when he threw homeward to nail runners trying to score, he never threw to the catcher. He threw to the umpire because the ump always positioned himself to see the slide at home. He felt it gave him an advantage because the ump could easily see the ball's arrival in front of his face.

E&J: Could anyone throw better than Clemente?

Art: No one. But Willie Mays had a throwing arm equal to Clemente's. Carl Furillo of the Dodgers also had a great throwing arm.

E&J: Let's get back to your career as the Buc public address announcer.

Art: It was a great experience. I remember introducing Vice President Richard Nixon. That was a great thrill for me. I remember Umpire Ed Sudol taking the time to call me from the field with every change in the 1974 All-Star Game lineup so that I would be correct and on top of things. It was difficult to be involved in a circus like the All-Star Game from the press box and not be connected with anyone down on the field. Sudol was so kind and helpful and I never forgot his assistance. I was very proud of doing both p.a. announcer and scoreboard operator simultaneously.

E&J: Who was your first Pirate hero?

Art: Babe Adams. I used to catch-in for him when he hit fungoes during fielding practice prior to the start of the games. That was the job of the pitchers when they were not pitching that day. Adams would stand to the right of home plate and hit the ball to right

and center fields. He would look around for me and call, "Where's my boy?" I'd run over and catch the throws back to him. In those days I was so proud to be near him. He was

Babe Adams, late in his Pirate career.

the pitching hero of the 1909 World Series, winning three games over the Tigers. He was from the state of Missouri, and he was a very calm and gentle person.

In fact, he had a heartbeat of only 58 beats per minute. He pitched a little in the 1925 World Series. He had a great year in 1921 winning 14 and losing just five. He and Whitey Glazner had great seasons for the Bucs in 1921. They had identical pitching records that year. Glazner, unfortunately, disappeared from baseball shortly thereafter.

E&J: What did you think of the Hall of Famer Arky Vaughan?

Art: He was just about as good a hitter as I ever saw. I do not know why it took so long for him to be voted into the Hall of Fame. He was an excellent hitter and a very good fielder. If he had any fielding problem, it was the slow grounder hit directly at him.

He was a very low-key person. I remember one time when Eddie Stanky of the Dodgers came sliding into second with his spikes a little high, and he nicked Vaughan. Stanky's hat flew off and Vaughan promptly kicked it into center field. He then told Stanky that he would kick **him** into center field the next time he came into second base like that. Vaughan was slow to anger, but once riled, he became a very tough kid.

E&J: .The destruction of Forbes Field must have been a serious loss to you personally.

Art: Right before the last doubleheader played at Forbes between the Bucs and the Cubs, I told everybody that I was going to stay in the park all night, like sitting up with a dying friend. I just wanted to look over the place for the last time. I really didn't want to leave. I wanted to hold the hand of my dying friend. That is how I felt.

I grew up at Forbes Field. I had been going there for more than 50 years, and it meant a great deal to me. However, the city needed an all-purpose stadium to house the Steelers in order to keep them here. The Steelers had never had their own field to play on. Seemingly, they were always "borrowing" Forbes Field or Pitt Stadium. I think that is why Three Rivers Stadium is better for viewing football than baseball. But it is plastic to me.

However, when we moved into the place in 1970, it was a joy because the working facilities were far superior to those of Forbes Field. Restaurants and toilet facilities were far better in the new park. The University [of Pittsburgh] had purchased Forbes Field from the Bucs, and just let it run down. Why would they put any money into it? It was scheduled for demolition, plain and simply. By 1970, it was totally tired and rundown.

The major regret I have with Three Rivers Stadium is that center field is not open for viewing the city the way the original plans called for. It would have cost a lot more money to open the stadium in center field than to close it the way they did. That seems strange to me.

E&J: Would real grass make you feel better about the stadium?

Art: No. The Steelers ruined the grounds at Forbes Field every year. They had to re-sod the field every spring. The place always looked like a patch quilt. The Steelers would do the same thing in Three Rivers Stadium. Putting in new sod every year is horribly expensive. Mayor Sophie Masloff had a great idea a few years ago when she suggested a separate baseball park for the Pirates. It was just ill-timed. However, they have it in Kansas City and other places.

E&J: Barney Dreyfuss ran a very tight ship in your early days with the Pirates.

Art: Indeed. In my early days, Dreyfuss, his son and the team treasurer ran the whole thing. They had just a handful of employees. I know it was less than ten. It seems hard to believe. They ran everything. Today, it seems to me that the Pirates have everybody in the world working for them. I see all those names in the press guide, and it staggers me. Wow!

E&J: How would you evaluate Branch Rickey's tenure with the Bucs?

Art: Rickey wanted young ballplayers in Pittsburgh. He also wanted them married as soon as possible. He wanted them concentrating on baseball and nothing else. He never fulfilled his Pittsburgh ambitions. He had been very successful in both St. Louis and Brooklyn, but not here.

He started farm system baseball in St. Louis, and controlled so many ballplayers that Judge Landis, I believe, had to break it up so that some of them could eventually make it to the majors. As I recall, Rickey was really one of the smartest baseball men ever. But, he would not go to the ball park on Sunday. He had promised his mother years before that he would keep the Lord's Day, and he did. He was well educated, and he lived and spoke the part. Unfortunately, perhaps, he did not stay very long in Pittsburgh.

E&J: If there is anyone who should know this, it is you, Art. Why did the Pirates retire Billy Meyer's number "1"?

Art: Because the Pirate organization truly loved the man. I have asked a number of people who should know, and they all said the organization was fond of him and always had been. They wanted to do him a special favor.

He had one great season as a Buc manager in 1948. The team was in contention for the pennant up to the final couple weeks. It lost to the Boston Braves with ex-Buc Bob Elliott leading the way. Meyer had Danny Murtaugh playing second and Stan Rojek playing short. Kiner was in left with Wally Westlake in center. Frankie Gustine played third. It was a very good team.

E&J: How well do you remember Dino Restelli?

Art: The greatest flash in the pan ever: 12 homers in 1949. It seemed like he hit them all in his first two or three weeks here. Chilly Doyle of the Pittsburgh *Sun-Telegraph* wrote a story about Restelli later that said he was not as good as his father's spaghetti. His dad owned a restaurant on the West Coast. Restelli was a lot like Johnny Rizzo, only Rizzo lasted longer. Vince DiMaggio was similar to both. Vince struck out with more style and poetry than any other righthanded batter I ever saw. He was beautiful.

E&J: What about some of the changes that you have seen in the game?

Art: What do you mean? The DH? Things like that? Oh, I dislike the DH. I am a purist. Do not change a thing. I even dislike the turf. However, the locker-rooms are much better today. You should have seen the Pirate clubhouse in those early days. It was just like a stable. It had a wooden floor with very large lockers for each player. A man could walk in and out of his locker. There was no carpeting. There was one big table in the middle of the room for cards and other things. The place always smelled of wintergreen. That is all the trainer used to treat the players for any and all ills.

No one has seen more Pirate baseball than Art McKennan.

That's all. However, he was not really a trainer. He was really a masseur. The strange thing was that nobody ever went on the disabled list in those days. Not like they do today.

E&J: During your public address days, what was the toughest name or thing to pronounce?

Art: Without a doubt, the name Ed Kranepool. No matter how I did it or tried my best to pronounce it correctly, it always sounded like Ed Kranepoooo. That final "L" was always a problem for me.

E&J: Who were your favorite all-time Pirates?

Art: My two favorites were Max Carey and Dick Groat. Carey walked like his legs were made of springs. He had marvelous legs, and he was very fast. Gosh, he stole better than sixty bases one season. Groat was a terrific money player, both hitting and fielding. I'll never forget watching Groat one day when he was playing against the Bucs in his waning big league days as a Phillie. He had a severe leg injury at the time, but stayed in the lineup. He was literally playing on one leg when he went into the hole between short and third. He made a backhand stab of a grounder and threw out a runner trying to score at home. At the time I thought that only Dick Groat could have made that play. He was pure guts.

E&J: You mentioned Negro baseball earlier. What do you recall now?

Art: In my early days Negro baseball here was really sandlot baseball. Sometimes those guys would play three games in a day, especially on holidays. They'd play a morning game and an afternoon game. And then they would play a game at Forbes Field after the Pirates finished their contest. I would see those guys so tired sometimes that they would not be wearing their baseball shoes, just slippers. A lot of times they would not take batting practice. They would just take the field and play. They had a lot of excellent players. They had Josh Gibson, Dick Harris, Oscar Charleston and Cool Papa Bell. My scoreboard friend and I would sit on the bench with them when they played at Forbes. We would coordinate the scoreboard for them. My friend and I were the only white people allowed to sit on the bench with the black players.

Cumberland Posey, who ran the Grays, was very nice to me. The Grays would draw crowds of 10 to 12 thousand people a game at Forbes Field. The crowds were mostly black people. They would play teams like the Monarchs and the Lincoln Giants at Forbes Field. They had their stars, and we had ours. They were good, and many of them could and should have played in the majors. There was one weak spot in Negro League baseball, and it was pitching. They did not really have pitching staffs. It seemed like everybody took a turn at pitching. The players were all-purpose players.

E&J: Who was the best player you ever saw?

Art: It is a toss-up between Clemente and Mays. However, my favorite manager of all time is the guy running the Pirates right now, Jim Leyland. The man is a psychologist. He treats people in the same way he wants to be treated, and the players love him. He follows the golden rule. He also plays all of his players, and they love that as well.

When the Champs Were No-Hit

You heard it here first

By Richard McBane

ON SUNDAY, AUGUST 22, 1926, the defending World Champion Pittsburgh Pirates were locked in a tight pennant race with the St. Louis Cardinals. That afternoon the Pirates fielded a lineup that included three future Hall of Famers. For their efforts, the Bucs were no-hit.

Neither the loss, nor the no-hitter, however, went into the record books because the Pirates weren't playing a National League team. They weren't even playing a team in the National Association. Instead, the Pirates lost to Charles E. Ketchum and the Akron Generals of the Ohio-Pennsylvania League, a semi-pro industrial circuit.

Sunday baseball was illegal in Pennsylvania in 1926. Pittsburgh had a Monday doubleheader on tap the next day against the Brooklyn Dodgers, but teams of that era seldom enjoyed an off-day. Akron was easily accessible by rail, so the Pirates boarded a train for their date with destiny.

As for the Hall-of-Fame lineup, Pittsburgh led off with Paul Waner in right field. Waner, a rookie, hit .336 that year with 35 doubles, 22 triples, 8 homers and 79 RBIs. Batting second was another rookie, shortstop Joe Cronin. While Waner was a regular, Cronin was a true rookie. He appeared in only 38 games for the Pirates that year and was in the lineup only because regular shortstop Glenn Wright was injured. The other Buc Hall of Famer was Pie Traynor, playing third and batting cleanup. He was on his way to a .317 average that year with 92 RBIs and a league-leading 182 put-outs by a third baseman. 1926 was the third time he led the National League in that stat; he would do it four more times to tie the all-time record.

The hurler who baffled them was a tall, thin, raw-boned 30-year-old righthander who was at the pinnacle of his career. Charlie Ketchum had bounced around the minor leagues. He'd left Columbus of the American Association earlier in 1926 to pitch for the Generals, and was a key factor in making them an industrial league power.

He had tossed a no-hitter for the Generals against New Castle of the Ohio-Pennsylvania League on the previous Sunday. Three days later he pitched a 6-0 five-hitter against Youngstown in another league game, extending his string of hitless innings to 13 before giving up a single through the box.

Ketchum, however, had a poorly kept secret. He scuffed the ball, apparently using emery dust stuck into a wad of chewing gum. Harold Sloop, an Akron high school boy trying to rehab his shoulder by pitching batting practice for the Generals, was on the field before the game. He overheard a conversation between the umpire and Pirate skipper Bill McKechnie. Sloop recalled:

"Before the game, the umpire (Red

Carney) told McKechnie that Ketchum cheated, and asked if McKechnie wanted him to call it. McKechnie said 'Let him throw.' He thought McKechnie may have regretted it later."

Whatever Ketchum threw that day, his General teammates gave him fine defensive support. Four fine fielding plays robbed the Pirates of possible hits. Until the ninth inning, only one Pittsburgh batter had reached base, and that on a shortstop error.

Akron scored in the first inning and clung to a 1-0 lead until the last of the seventh when they gave Ketchum some breathing room. With two outs in the top of the ninth Waner came to the plate. Leading 6-0, Ketchum decided to play the odds and protect the no-hitter. He issued an intentional walk to Waner in order to pitch to Cronin. Ketchum induced Cronin to ground out, ending the game.

Not surprisingly, Akron sports writers touted Ketchum as a future big leaguer. His two no-hitters in eight days attracted the attention of scouts.— for about a week. The following Sunday, Ketchum pitched another exhibition against the Boston Braves and lost 7-5. He never reached the big time.

Ketchum became a golf pro in 1928, serving several public courses around Akron and one in Toledo. But he also liked to drink and he soon fell on hard times. Subsequently, he had some run-ins with the law. In addition, in February 1934, in just his second day of work as a coal truck driver, he was struck by a trailer while unloading coal on Akron's East Market Street. Ketchum died at his parents' home in Akron in October 1944. He was 48.

As for the 1926 Pirates, they finished third.

This box score is compiled from those published in the Pittsburgh Gazette Times, The Pittsburgh Press and Akron Beacon Journal. Each of the three published boxes was slightly different with some players omitted.

Pirates	AB	R	H	P	A	Gen. Tires	AB	R	H	P	A
Waner rf	3	0	0	0	0	Savage lf	4	1	1	1	0
Cronin ss	4	0	0	2	2	Hassel'n ss	4	0	0	3	2
Barnhart cf	3	0	0	0	0	Darling rf	3	1	1	3	0
Traynor 3b	3	0	0	1	3	Snyder 1b	4	0	0	14	0
McInnis 1b	3	0	0	12	0	Mostade 2b	4	1	1	1	2
Brickell lf	3	0	0	0	0	Messner 3b	4	1	2	0	7
Rawlings 2b	2	0	0	1	1	Graham cf	4	1	2	2	0
Spencer c	3	0	0	6	0	Doherty c	3	1	1	3	1
Morrison p	1	0	0	0	1	Ketchum p	3	0	1	0	1
Nichols p	1	0	0	1	2						
Rhyne 2b	1	0	0	1	4						
Murphy ph	1	0	0	0	0						
Ens 3b	0	0	0	0	2						
Totals	28	0	0	24	15	Totals	33	6	9	27	13

Pittsburgh   0 0 0 0 0 0 0 0 0 - 0
Akron   1 0 0 0 0 0 2 3 x - 6

Errors - Traynor, Hasselman, Spencer, Barnhart. Two-base hits - Mostade. Stolen bases - Savage, Graham. Sacrifice hits - Doherty. Bases on balls - Off Nichols 1, off Ketchum 1. Struck out - By Morrison 4, by Ketchum 3, by Nichols 2. Wild pitch by Nichols. One run, 2 hits off Morrison in 3 innings; off Nichols 5 runs, 7 hits in 6 innings. Time of game 1:13. Umpires - Red Carney and Kubat.

Another Side of 'Bobby' Clemente

Long-time Buc trainer Tony Bartirome remembers a fun-loving, playful man

By Norman L. Macht

THERE WAS A SIDE TO Bobby Clemente—as most NL players called him in the 1960s—that the press and public never saw: Clemente was one of the most entertaining jokesters and storytellers in the clubhouse.

"He was the funniest man I every saw in there," Tony Bartirome, the long-time trainer, told me as we sat in the bleachers at the old spring training ballpark in Bradenton. "But he was that way only among the players. As soon as the writers came in, he clammed up. They never saw it.

"He had a knack of getting the team up, if they were in a slump, by making everybody relax and feel good. You always found him at the center of the noise and life and laughter."

Bill Virdon, Clemente's last manager in 1972, agreed. "You got him going on a plane or bus telling jokes and stories and he had everybody in stitches."

Bobby and his wax duplicate. Can you identify the real Clemente?

Clemente was proud of the six months he spent in the Marine reserves. All somebody had to do was ask him about it, and he would go into an hour-long act describing the experience down to the last detail.

One of his favorite stories involved the practical joke they played on the team doctor. There was a life-size wax statue of Clemente in the Pirates' front office. One day Bartirome carried it into the clubhouse.

"I took it into an empty room adjacent to the clubhouse," the trainer recalled. "It was dark and shadowy and very cold in there. The only light in the room came from a nearby bathroom. I laid it on a platform and covered it to the chin with a blanket while the players watched. Then I called the doctor and told him, 'Bobby's real sick, Doc, you better come and do something. We put him in the side room in case the writers came in.'"

The doctor came and touched the statue's hand; it was cold as ice. Concerned, he put his ear to the chest. Failing to detect a heartbeat, he cried, "My God, he's dead!"

The players crowding the doorway erupted with laughter that gave away the prank.

"Every time I told that story," Bartirome said, "Bobby would stand there listening and beaming."

In addition to his sense of humor, Clemente was known among the players as a kind and considerate person. He went out of his way to speak to the wives and children of employees at the ballpark whenever he saw them. His kindnesses extended to players on other teams. One snowy winter night he and Richie Ashburn shared the spotlight at a banquet.

"After it was over he offered to drive me to the airport," Ashburn recalled. "The snow was deep on the roads. I figured it was on his way, so I said okay. I found out later that he was really going to the other side of the city and it was far out of his way."

Public appearances often netted star players $500 or more in those days; the "other" guys on the team seldom got invited. One day Clemente called a team meeting. He proposed that all speaking fees be pooled and divided up among all the players at the end of the year. But he could not get a unanimous agreement. After that, he agreed to appear only if a lesser-known player was also invited, and the two of them would split the fees.

Television commercials offered big paychecks to stars. Once, Clemente agreed to appear on one in which other players also appeared in the background at much lower fees. When he discovered how much less they were being paid, he demanded that all the players be paid the same as he was getting. The sponsor refused; Clemente turned down the job.

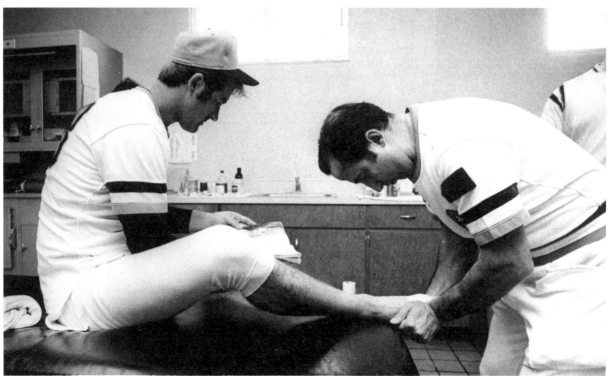

Buc trainer Bartirome works on the foot of Steve Blass while Steve studies.

The Best Player-Seasons in Pirate History

A Statistical Evaluation

By Neal D. Traven

WHO ARE THE BEST PLAYERS in the history of the Pirates? Everyone responding to that question will, of course, approach it differently. Some may rely on their personal recollections of thrilling plays and great moments, others might look at old newspapers and read about World Series exploits, and still others will review the record books and encyclopedias.

In this article, I'll try to do the job "scientifically," removing as many biases and preconceptions as possible, and specifying the methods of analysis and the assumptions used in the evaluation. I'll be using "state of the art" sabrmetric tools, some of which have been developed, discussed, and honed on the Internet but haven't been seen much in print.

Before starting, let's consider for a moment what "best" really means. Should we look at a player's *career* accomplishments with the Bucs or his value at his *peak*? Neither viewpoint is superior to the other, and both can offer interesting results. I've decided to present peak performances in this article — the best *single seasons* generated by players for the Pirates. Similar methodology will be applied to Pirate *careers* in a research presentation at the Pittsburgh SABR convention.

Ground rules

Pete Palmer kindly provided season-by-season data for the 1420 men who played National League baseball in Pittsburgh in the 108 years between 1887 and 1994. I'm looking solely at their records *with the Pirates*, a total of 3712 season records.

The primary tool employed in this analysis is Clay Davenport's *Equivalent Runs* (EqR) approach. A hitter's EqR is the estimated number of runs that he added to the league's total for the year. Sabrmetricians are interested in estimating runs because that is the "currency" of baseball — games are won by scoring more runs than the opponents do. The team's hitters try to maximize runs scored, and simultaneously the pitchers try to minimize runs allowed.

The methodology adjusts EqR for *year effects* and *park effects*. Using the currency metaphor, a year effect is like monetary inflation (in high-offense years, each additional run is less "valuable" than in normal years.) Year effects include such broad concepts as the "deadball" and "lively ball" eras, the "pitchers' year" of 1968, and last year's offensive explosion. Park effects are like the disparity in cost-of-living between, say, New York City and a farm community. With Colorado's entry into the big leagues, many people have noted its extreme pro-offense park effect. The negative effect of, for example, Forbes Field on homers is much less noticed. Park effects vary from year to year, often due to moved fences — in the Greenberg Gardens/Kiner's Korner years, Forbes Field was nearly neutral for home runs.

Adjusting for those effects places the

estimate of a player's runs (now called EPER) in a common context, a hypothetical neutral park in the 1992 American League. The specific league-season isn't what's important, though; the significance is that the adjusted stats are *directly comparable* — there's no need to worry about whether it's 1930 or 1968, Baker Bowl or Dodger Stadium. It's analogous to the familiar procedure of adjusting for inflation by expressing all prices in, say, "1990 dollars."

A similar approach is used to place pitching statistics in a common context. Because the structure of pitching staffs has changed so radically over the last century, individual innings pitched were adjusted to approximate the 1992 AL's distribution, with the adjustment based on the league's #2 and #4 pitchers in IP. For example, Pud Galvin's 440.2 IP in 1887 were adjusted to 262.1 IP in this analysis. The measure used for ranking pitchers was "runs saved," defined as the difference between the total runs allowed by the pitcher (using his adjusted innings and adjusted ERA) and the number of runs allowed by an "average" pitcher — one whose ERA was 4.00 — in the same number of innings. Thus, both quality (ERA) and quantity (innings) go into the measure.

For pitchers, individual batting and fielding were not used in the rankings. For the rest of the players, however, it was important to measure defense, even knowing that fielding measures are far less powerful than those for hitting and pitching.

The best way to assess fielding is to determine how many balls hit in a player's direction he actually gets to. Only since Project Scoresheet, and its stepchildren STATS, Inc. and The Baseball Workshop, began to collect such data in 1988 has it been possible to compute such a measure. STATS produces its Zone Rating, and Sherri Nichols of SABR calculates Defensive Average (DA).

The two are similar in their focus. They're vastly more useful than any previous fielding assessments, all of which are flawed because they consider only *chances accepted,* so a ball that might have been handled by a better fielder is called a hit, and not charged in any way against the immobile fielder. Perhaps the least problematical of previous rankings is Palmer's linear weights-based Fielding Runs, which is used here for the years 1887-1987. For 1988-1994, Dale Stephenson's Fielding Runs statistic (based on the Nichols DA data) is the measure of defense. It must be noted that catcher defense remains all but completely inscrutable. Palmer uses team ERA as one of the components of his rating, and DA simply ignores catchers.

Players were assessed only at their primary positions for the season, and only seasons where the player spent at least half of his defensive games at the primary position were considered (this condition affected the composition of the roster at only one position). While the complete batting record was used, fielding only at the primary position was included in the overall rating of a player. The final ranking for non-pitchers was based on the number of runs the player generated, compared to what an "average" player would have produced while consuming the same number of outs. Two players made the roster at each position.

To demonstrate the process, consider Lloyd Waner's rookie year of 1927. Little Poison set the all-time record for hits by a rookie with 223 and compiled a .355/.396/.410 (BA/OBP/SP) mark. He added 102 EqR to the NL that year; adjusting for Forbes Field (a hitters' park but not a homerun park) and the high offense of the season decreases him to an EPER of 94, or 97 in a 162-game season. Lloyd's glove was poor that year, -11 FR. Adjusted to a neutral 162-game season, that's -10 FR, so his total for the season is 87 runs produced. An average 1927 player making 406 outs would have accumulated 75 EqR, which adjusts to 72 EPER, plus zero Fielding Runs.

Therefore, after all adjustments Lloyd Waner produced only about 15 (87-72) runs more than an average player. Which is about the same as say, Billy Sunday in 1888 or Mike Easler in 1982.

The players

Leading off for the Pirates' seasonal all-time team is centerfielder **Max Carey, 1917**. Though he hit just .296/.369/.378 for the cellar-dwelling Bucs, it came in one of the deadest of the deadball years. Carey's superb fielding also contributed mightily. Just a bit behind Carey is **Andy Van Slyke, 1988**; though Slick hit a bit better in 1992, his once-fine fielding had deteriorated significantly by then. Ginger Beaumont, 1902, is next in line among Pirate CFs.

Our number two hitter is surely the least-known player on the roster, third baseman **Jimmy Williams, 1899**. Has anyone, anywhere, had a better rookie year than his spectacular .355/.416/.532 numbers? Williams, who had never before had even a cup of coffee in the bigs, led the league in triples and finished in the top five in seven other batting categories that year. He played just two years for the Bucs, jumping to Baltimore in 1901 and spending the rest of his career in the American League. Williams even fielded deftly enough to move to second base, which he played quite well, for most of his career. His backup is **Tommy Leach, 1902,** who combined fine fielding and solid power (he led the league in both triples and homers). The 1923 season of Hall of Famer Pie Traynor, who most readers would have expected to man this position, came in a year of high offense. His good but not great fielding left him behind the underappreciated Leach. Indifferent fielding put Bill Madlock, 1981, out of the running.

The only unknown at shortstop on this team is which **Honus Wagner** season ranks highest. As it turns out, **1908** was a poor glove year for the Dutchman, but his .354/.410/.542

absolutely towered over the worst year for offense in National League history. Fred Tenney of the Giants scored one more run, Brooklyn's Tim Jordan hit a couple more homers, and Wagner didn't walk very much; otherwise, Honus led the league in everything, often by a hefty margin (an astonishing 90 points in slugging percentage). **Arky Vaughan, 1935**, took the runnerup spot at shortstop (well, runnerup behind *seven* more Wagner seasons), and his 1938 season, when he fielded extremely well, was almost as good. The two — unquestionably the best shortstop of all time, and a plausible choice for second-best — dominate the position, of course. Jay Bell, 1993, shows up on the list behind ten Wagner and four Vaughan seasons, with another Wagner and four more Vaughans between Bell and Dick Groat, 1960.

Batting cleanup, with undoubtedly the finest season ever compiled by a Pirate not named Wagner, is leftfielder **Barry Bonds, 1992**. He did it all with the bat (.311/.457/.624 in a year when the National League was weak on offense), more than compensating for a merely good season afield. Barry's 1990 season was nearly as good — his hitting wasn't as great but he had an exceptional fielding year. He's is in some very strong company, however. The huge difference between Bonds' glove and his own subpar fielding kept **Ralph Kiner, 1949**, out of the top spot in left; at the plate, Kiner put up superior numbers. And Willie Stargell, 1973, was close on Kiner's heels.

Rightfielder **Roberto Clemente, 1967**, bats fifth in this lineup. The Great One combined the National League batting title, in a low-offense year, with splendid defense. The difference between the pitching-dominated '60s and the lively ball '20s is evident when you look at his backup — **Paul Waner, 1927**, had much better raw numbers and was also a fine fielder, but his adjusted results didn't quite match Clemente's. Dave Parker, 1977, (an extraordinary year with the glove) and

Kiki Cuyler, 1925, (in his only rightfield season as a Buc), also fine fielders, couldn't quite match Clemente and Waner.

Batting sixth is first baseman **Elbie Fletcher, 1941**. With all the superb outfielders the Pirates have showcased over the years, it's surprising that first base has been such a weak position for the club. Fletcher had good gap power, drew tons of walks, and played fine defense, but he was nowhere near the level of the Bucs manning the other "offensive" positions on this roster. Backing him up is another big surprise, **Bob Robertson, 1971**, whose talents were muted by the low-offense era he played in.

How weak has first base been in Bucco history? After Robertson come Jason Thompson, 1982, and slick-fielding Sid Bream, 1986. Hall of Famer Jake Beckley, playing in the high-offense 1890s, was well down on the list.

Catcher **Tony Pena, 1984**, hits in the seventh spot for the club. In a low-offense year, catching the league's best pitching staff (this was the season in which the Pirates led in ERA while finishing dead last), Pena takes the starting position ahead of **Manny Sanguillen, 1975**. It should be pointed out that two long-ago Pirate backstops, Fred Carroll, 1889, and Doggie Miller, 1891, who would have ranked first and fourth, respectively, were eliminated from consideration due to our requirement of playing at least 50% of the season's defensive games at his primary position. Carroll played 43 games at C, 41 in the OF, seven at 1B, and one at 3B (and was actually the 1889 backup to Miller). In 1891, Miller played 37 games at SS, 34 games at 3B, 24 games in the OF, and one at 1B along with his 41 games behind the plate. Those guys could hit, but they don't quite seem like fulltime catchers.

By far the greatest impact of adding a measure of defense to the evaluation process appears at second base. Looking only at hit-

ting, unknown Jim Viox, 1913, who seems to have known very little about what to do with that leather thing he had to wear between plate appearances, topped the Bucco list. He was followed by George Grantham, 1930, Dots Miller, 1909, and Johnny Ray, 1984, all known for fielding ineptitude. Meanwhile, arguably the finest fielder in the history of the game, at *any* position, played many years of 2B for the Pirates. Our number eight hitter, then, is **Bill Mazeroski, 1963**, whose fielding brilliance (in that and several other seasons) outshines every other Bucco second sacker. Another good field/no hit player, **Pep Young, 1938**, is Maz's backup.

The pitchers

With all that firepower among the hitters (Traynor, Lloyd Waner, Stargell, Cuyler, Clarke, Beckley, Lindstrom — Hall of Famers all — didn't make the club), you probably don't need to depend on good pitching. That's fortunate, because, to be frank about it, the Pirates have been weak in that department throughout their history. No pitcher has ever been elected to the Hall of Fame because of his feats with the Bucs; newly-chosen Vic Willis probably comes the closest, though most of his prime years were spent with the Braves.

I couldn't decide whether to carry five starters and four relievers, or vice versa, so let's just expand the team's roster by one, presenting the five-man starting rotation and five-man relief corps for the Bucs' seasonal all-time team. As described earlier, pitchers are ranked by the total number of runs they saved the team in comparison with an "average" pitcher (defined as 4.00 adjusted ERA) in the same number of innings. This measure accounts for both quality of pitching (low ERA) and quantity of pitching (maintaining that ERA over more innings will save the club more runs). Note, however, that innings pitched for the early years of the game are adjusted to current-day practices — no 440-inning seasons for Pud Galvin and friends.

The very best season by a Pirate starting pitcher, **Preacher Roe, 1945**, seems worthy of extended study. Even if we discount it as a war-year anomaly, an analysis of the run support differences between Roe and the other starters on the club would be instructive. How else to explain how a pitcher who saved his team nearly 40 runs over the course of the season, on a club finishing 10 games over .500, who led the league in strikeouts and had pinpoint control, whose estimated record with an average offense in a neutral park in a neutral year would be 19-8, ended up as a 14-13 pitcher? Whatever happened to Roe certainly didn't affect teammate Nick Strincevich, who went 16-10 with an ERA half a run higher.

Following Roe are pitchers much more commonly associated with the Bucs. **Babe Adams, 1913**, was the best of many solid years for the leading hurler of the deadball era Bucs. Similarly, **Vernon Law, 1959**, and **Bob Friend, 1955**, were prime performances by the pitching stalwarts of the legendary 1960 World Series champs, and **Rick Rhoden, 1986**, capped the Pirate career of a pitcher who re-established himself during the gloomy mid-1980s.

Close behind this quintet are Rick Reuschel, 1985, a brilliant season with too few innings to join the rotation, Bob Veale, 1964, and Wilbur Cooper, 1922.

The indisputable ace of the bullpen spent just one season as a member of the Pirates, but what a year it was! Only eleven seasons by *starting* pitchers have ever saved the Bucs more runs than **Goose Gossage, 1977**, and most of them needed about twice as many innings to do it. The rest of the bullpen on the club includes **Roy Face, 1962** (not the year he went 18-1), **Kent Tekulve, 1983, Al McBean, 1964**, and **Bill Landrum, 1989**. All five relievers are righthanded; Rod Scurry, 1982, and Ramon Hernandez, 1973, are the best of a rather weak collection of southpaw relievers.

Conclusions

Undoubtedly, most of you find some of my selections to be ridiculous or silly. I tried to carry out these analyses with as few preconceptions and as few biases as possible, letting the numbers speak for themselves. None of the people whose analyses I employed — Davenport, Palmer, Nichols, Stephenson — try to steer their results in any way; we're all interested only in trying to assess what the documentary record of baseball tells us about the game.

Still, there are assuredly flaws in the models or the reasoning involved in the systems developed for this analysis. There is always room for improvement, and everyone involved in this project would be delighted to hear constructive criticisms or to discover additional raw data that would enhance the methodology. The deficiencies in our knowledge base are far greater when it comes to fielding than any other aspect, but evaluation of hitting and pitching data can always stand improvement as well.

Along with the researchers whose work I've used in these analyses, I thank David Tate, David Grabiner, and many others on the Internet and elsewhere for their assistance and guidance in this project.

The Best Buc Single Seasons

			Actual				Year/Park Adjusted			
										Above
Player, Year	Pos	BA	OBA	SLG	EqR	FR	EPER	FR	Total	Avg.
Barry Bonds 1992	LF	.311	.457	.624	132	4	150	5	155	97
Max Carey 1917	CF	.296	.369	.378	92	20	113	25	138	65
R. Clemente 1967	RF	.357	.402	.554	121	8	136	9	145	82
Elbie Fletcher 1941	1B	.288	.421	.457	108	9	113	9	122	58
Ralph Kiner 1949	LF	.310	.432	.658	153	-4	151	-4	147	80
Tommy Leach 1902	3B	.278	.341	.426	88	13	107	16	123	51
Bill Mazeroski 1963	2B	.245	.288	.343	53	57	62	67	130	59
Tony Pena 1984	C	.286	.334	.425	75	12	87	14	101	28
R.Robertson 1971	1B	.271	.358	.484	79	15	90	17	107	47
M.Sanguillen 1975	C	.328	.393	.451	81	-5	89	-5	83	26
A.Van Slyke 1988	CF	.288	.352	.506	105	11	124	13	137	62
Arky Vaughan 1935	SS	.385	.485	.607	144	-11	135	-10	124	71
H.Wagner 1908	SS	.354	.410	.542	132	-7	185	-10	175	105
Paul Waner 1927	RF	.380	.437	.549	142	9	135	9	144	76
J.Williams 1899	3B	.355	.416	.532	158	7	135	6	141	68
Pep Young 1938	2B	.278	.329	.381	72	32	77	34	111	36

			Actual			Year/Park Adjusted			
									Runs
Pitcher, Year	S/R/Th	IP	ERA	W-L		IP	ERA	W-L	Saved
Babe Adams 1913	SP R	313.2	2.15	21-10		252.1	2.68	19-9	37
Roy Face 1962	RP R	91	1.88	8-7		84	2.04	7-2	18
Bob Friend 1955	SP R	200.1	2.83	14-9		212	2.63	17-7	32
Rich Gossage 1977	RP R	133	1.62	11-9		118.2	1.90	11-2	28
Bill Landrum 1989	RP R	81	1.67	2-3		82.2	2.18	7-2	17
Vernon Law 1959	SP R	266	2.98	18-9		245.2	2.67	19-8	36
Al McBean 1964	RP R	89.2	1.91	8-3		79.1	2.04	7-2	17
Rick Rhoden 1986	SP R	253.2	2.84	15-12		246.	2.85	18-9	31
Preacher Roe 1945	SP L	235	2.87	14-13		242.1	2.53	19-8	40
Kent Tekulve 1983	RP R	99	1.64	7-5		94	2.30	8-2	18

Key

BA = Batting average, **OB** = On-base percentage, **SLG**= Slugging percentage

EqR = Equivalent Runs (unadjusted)

FR = Fielding Runs (linear weights 1887-1987, DA-based 1988-1994)

EPER = EqR adjusted for park, year, and length of season

Above Avg.= number of runs above what an 'average' player would do while consuming the same number of outs

Rs (Runs) Saved = difference between the pitcher's own (adjusted) runs allowed and the number allowed by an average pitcher in the same number of (adjusted) innings

Pittsburgh and the Negro Leagues

A grand and glorious tradition

By Rob Ruck

NOTE: A version of this article appeared in Pittsburgh *magazine, February, 1993.*

WITH COOL PAPA BELL FLYING around the base paths, Josh Gibson drawing accolades as the black Babe Ruth, and Satchel Paige walking the bases loaded, telling his fielders to sit down, and striking out the side, Pittsburgh was once the center of a black baseball world that stretched from Chicago to the Caribbean.

During the 1930s and '40s, when baseball was still divided by race, the black game was based in Pittsburgh. Headquarters to the Negro National League and home to the Pittsburgh Crawfords and the Homestead Grays, Pittsburgh fielded an array of stars.

The Grays and the Crawfords dominated black baseball, winning 13 Negro League pennants between them in 16 seasons and sending seven players to the Hall of Fame. Club owners Cumberland Posey , Jr. and Gus Greenlee helped build baseball into the third biggest black business in the nation (after the black insurance companies and the numbers game — a forerunner of the lottery).

They did so in spite of, and in part because of, segregation. And when segregation in baseball ended, so did these autonomous black leagues. Black baseball's story is more than a tale of athletic grace amid a tortured racial setting. It highlights what black America created on its own during this epoch and how much was lost when integration brought about

black baseball's demise.

Driven out of integrated baseball by rising racial intolerance in the 1890s, African-Americans turned inward and created a league of their own that stretched across a swath of northern cities. Because of geography and the nation's fifth largest black population in 1930, Pittsburgh became the crossroads for black teams. Passing through the city meant playing the Homestead Grays, a club begun in 1900 by black workers in the Monongahela mill town.

By the end of World War I, the Grays had become the best sandlot team in the region. The catalyst to their ascent was Homestead native Cumberland Posey, an exceptional athlete who made the transition from player to promoter. Posey joined the Grays as an outfielder in 1911 and became the club's manager and owner by the 1920s. To a core of stellar locals, he added some of the best ballplayers in the country, including Oscar Charleston and Smokey Joe Williams.

By 1930, Cumberland Posey had transformed the Grays from a squad of steelworkers into the champions of black baseball. But on the sandlots of the Hill district of Pittsburgh, a challenger emerged — the Pittsburgh Crawfords.

Formed in 1925 by a dozen boys who lived on the Hill, the Crawfords took their name from the Crawford Bath House, which sponsored them in a city tournament. By the end of the decade, bolstered by the addition of several players from the Edgar Thomson Steelworks team, the Crawfords were ready to challenge the Grays.

Anchoring the club was catcher Josh Gibson, a strapping youth who had come north from Georgia when his father found work in one of Andrew Carnegie's mills. Gibson lasted but a few seasons with the Crawfords before Cum Posey offered him a spot in the Grays' lineup. There, at only 18 years of age, Gibson hit what might have been the first ball to clear the center field wall of Forbes Field.

As the Crawfords prepared to take on the Grays, a new force entered the city's sporting life. Numbers baron Gus Greenlee owned the Crawford Grill. He and Woogie Harris, a friend and associate who owned the Crystal Barbershop across the street from the grill, had made the numbers into the biggest business in black Pittsburgh. They gave part of their profits back to the community in the form of subsidies for sport and never-to-be-repaid loans to those in need.

When the Crawfords asked Greenlee to take over the club in 1930, Gus put the players on salary and set out to make them into the best black team ever. Greenlee lured Josh Gibson back from the Grays, and also took first baseman Oscar Charleston and third baseman Judy Johnson from Posey's club. James Cool Papa Bell, a slender young man from Mississippi who was considered by many the fastest baserunner ever, was signed to patrol center field. Greenlee also brought a lanky right-handed pitcher named Leroy Robert Satchel Paige to town. All five players ended up in the Hall of Fame.

Greenlee built the finest black-owned ballpark in the country on Bedford Avenue in the Hill and called it Greenlee Field. He resurrected the Negro National League, which had collapsed in 1931, and put its offices above the Crawford Grill.

Hall of Famer and former Negro Leaguer Monte Irvin calls the Crawfords black baseball's answer to the 1927 New York Yankees, thought to be the best major league team ever. Champions of the Negro National League in 1933, 1935, and 1936, the Crawfords were on the verge of being a baseball dynasty when the volatile politics of a Caribbean isle intruded.

While the Crawfords were in New Orleans for spring training in 1937, an emissary of Dominican Republic dictator Rafael Trujillo appeared. He offered Satchel Paige more money than even Greenlee was willing to pay if the pitcher would jump the Crawfords to play for Ciudad Trujillo in the Dominican.

Paige took the pesos and boarded Pan American's biplane to the islands. Gibson, Bell, and a half dozen other Crawfords soon joined him. Ciudad Trujillo vanquished its tropical opponents that summer, but what was left of the Crawfords fell into the second division. Greenlee relinquished the franchise a year later. Greenlee Field was torn down, replaced by the Bedford Dwellings housing project.

Although Paige never played for a Pittsburgh club again, Josh Gibson wound up back on the Grays. There, he teamed with Hall-of-Fame first baseman Buck Leonard as the Grays won the Negro National League pennant every year from 1937 until 1945.

During the late 1930s and World War II, the Grays played three games a week at Griffith Stadium in Washington D.C., where they often outdrew the white American League team. Black baseball finally achieved financial success, but the good times did not last long.

In the wake of the war, the struggle for integration converged with the major leagues' search for new fans and talent. In October 1945, Brooklyn Dodger President

Branch Rickey signed Negro League shortstop Jackie Robinson to a contract with the Dodgers' Montreal farm club. After a season in the minors, Robinson entered the majors in April, 1947. The color line was history.

Baseball's great experiment was a resounding success, both on the field and in its impact elsewhere in society. But there was a price — the end of the Negro Leagues.

"After Jackie," sighs Buck Leonard, "we couldn't draw flies." Deserted by their fans and the black press, and losing its best players to the major leagues, usually without compensation, the Negro National League folded in 1948. The Negro American League fell apart a few years later.

Mal Goode, the nation's first black television correspondent, concedes, "Integration had its disadvantages," including the end of black ownership. But Jackie Robinson opened doors of opportunity outside baseball. Likening the game's desegregation to that of schools, Goode concludes that though there were costs to pay, "What we gained was the greater — we got our self-respect back — and you have to have been black to understand what that meant."

For award-winning authors John Edgar Wideman and August Wilson, the end of the Negro Leagues was a harbinger of larger, and not always optimum, changes. "What was contained in those institutions," Wideman says of black baseball and colleges, "was not simply a black version of what white people were doing... and rather than having those institutions change the total picture, change what we all do, we lost them... That's not what integration is supposed to be about."

In 1948, the Homestead Grays won the last Negro World Series ever played, beating the Birmingham Black Barons. The league collapsed after the season and the Grays and their brethren soon became baseball's forgotten men. Black owners, general managers, and managers disappeared from the game. Black players, though, moved to baseball's center stage in the 1950s and '60s.

It is fitting that the Pittsburgh Pirates became the first major league club to honor the Negro Leagues. On a late summer night in 1988, the banner of the Homestead Grays flew over Three Rivers Stadium as the Pirates celebrated the 40th anniversary of the Grays' championship in the last Negro League World Series.

A. Bartlett Giamatti spoke to Doron Levin of *The New York Times* about the event. "We must never lose sight of our history," the late commissioner said, "insofar as it is ugly, never to repeat it, and insofar as it is glorious, to cherish it."

Pittsburgh has much to remember, and even more to cherish.

The Forbes Field Catch They Talked About 40 Years Later

Giant Red Murray made a grab with a flash

By Dan Bonk and Jay Gauthreaux

WHILE FORBES FIELD had its share of legendary home runs — Mazeroski's 1960 Game 7 World Series clout and Babe Ruth's final three — the old park was the scene of some memorable defensive moments as well: unassisted triple plays by Pirate shortstop Glenn Wright on May 7, 1925 and Cub shortstop Jimmy Cooney on May 30, 1927; and the bare-handed catch made by New York Giant right fielder Red Murray on August 16, 1909.

Murray's grab is the least-remembered today, because it happened nearly 90 years ago and none of its principals are alive to retell it. But the story was a familiar favorite more than 40 years after it took place. The Gene-Mack-style renderings of Forbes Field from the 1950s usually depict an "x" marking the spot where Murray made his dramatic grab; and no less than Honus Wagner frequently cited it as the greatest catch he ever saw.

In August of 1909, the Pirates were playing better than .700 ball and had healthy leads over the second-place Cubs (defending world champions), and the third-place New York Giants. On August 16, John McGraw's Giants visited Forbes Field and staked their ace, Christy Mathewson, to a 2-0 second-inning lead. But Buc hurler Vic Willis, Hall of Fame class of 1995, was equal to the task and kept the Pirates close.

In the bottom of the eighth inning, the Giants were clinging to a 2-1 lead. A strong wind began to swirl around the field. The crowd of roughly 11,000 could see a threatening sky approaching from the direction of Schenley Park, beyond the outfield wall.

Wily veteran Mathewson stalled, hoping that the oncoming storm would douse the game with his team in the lead. Legendary umpire Bill Klem ordered the bottom of the eighth to begin, prompting Pirate manager Fred Clarke to bat his pinch-hitting specialist Ham Hyatt for Willis. Mathewson delivered the first ball as a crash of thunder bellowed and a zig-zag flash of lightning lit the darkening grandstands. Hyatt met the ball and swatted a ringing triple to right field. The fireworks in the sky and on the field were followed by a brief lull during which Ed Abbaticchio was sent in to pinch run for Hyatt. Mathewson did his best to kill time but while the rain patiently held back, Abbaticchio came around to score on a Jap Barbeau sacrifice fly.

With the score tied the storm's approach was heralded by multiple thunderous booms. The next batter, Tommy Leach, belted a double to right. Hall of Famers-to-be Fred Clarke and Honus Wagner were coming up. The winds kicked up so much dust that the players were barely discernible from the stands. Large rain drops began to fall.

Mathewson induced Clarke to pop out weakly to short and with first base open, Wagner was intentionally walked. With two outs, two on, and the sky near bursting, Dots Miller strode to the plate. In the darkness, Mathewson's pitches were difficult to see, but Miller met one squarely and drove it into deep right center. Center fielder Cy Seymour and right fielder Red Murray sprinted in all-out pursuit.

From the stands the ball looked to be heading for the wall, a home run or at least a two-run triple. Seymour pulled up, apparently losing sight of the ball. Murray continued into the gap at full speed, stretched his bare right hand as far as he could, and snared the sailing liner just as another lightning bolt cracked behind him, framing his body in light.

Years later, Mathewson recalled, the accompanying crash of thunder "fairly jarred the earth." The inning and the rally were over in dramatic fashion. The deluge arrived. Soon the game was called, ending as a 2-2 tie.

Accounts of the game the following day profiled Murray's grab with descriptions such as marvelous, wonderful, and magnificent. *The Pittsburgh Leader* proclaimed in a headline, "Murray's Catch Greatest Ever Made on Ball Field," explaining that the play as well as the scene, "will never be duplicated."

More than a few eyebrows rose in disbelief when Honus Wagner told the story of Red Murray's lightning-lit catch to those who would listen. Sportswriter Sid Mercer, a founder of the Baseball Writers Association of America, nevertheless gave it credence. Mercer recalled that in later years the New York Giants re-enacted the miraculous bare-hand catch on Pullman cars. With the large lamps of the train car dimmed, Murray would pose as though he were snagging the Miller line drive, while somebody struck a match behind him, silhouetting his form just the way the lightning had in Forbes Field.

New York	ab	h	po	a	Pittsburgh	ab	h	po	a
Larry Doyle, 2b	4	2	1	1	Wm. Barbeau, 3b	3	1	1	0
Cy Seymour, cf	3	0	2	0	Tommy Leach, cf	4	1	1	0
Moose McCormick, lf	4	1	3	0	Fred Clarke, lf	4	0	3	0
Red Murray, rf	4	0	2	1	Honus Wagner, ss	3	1	5	0
Art Devlin, 3b	3	0	0	1	Dots Miller, 2b	4	1	2	4
Al Bridwell, ss	2	2	2	1	Bill Abstein, 1b	2	0	8	2
Fred Merkle, 1b	2	1	13	0	Owen Wilson, rf	3	0	1	0
Chief Meyers, c	2	0	1	1	George Gibson, c	3	2	2	4
Christy Mathewson, p	3	0	0	6	Vic Willis, p	2	0	1	4
					A- Ham Hyatt	1	1	0	0
					B - Ed Abbaticchio	0	0	0	0
TOTALS	27	6	24	11		29	7	24	14

A—Tripled for Willis in 8th. B—Ran for Hyatt in 8th.

New York	0	2	0	0	0	0	0	0	--	2
Base hits	1	1	0	1	0	1	1	1	--	6

Pittsburgh	0	0	1	0	0	0	0	1	--	2
Base hits	0	1	2	1	1	0	0	2	--	7

R — Gibson, Abbaticchio, Murray, Devlin. **E** — Barbeau, Clarke, Abstein. **2B** — Leach.
3B — Gibson, Hyatt. **Sacrifice Hits** — Bridwell, Merkle, Seymour. **Sac Fly** — Barbeau.
DP — Murray and Merkle. **LOB** —Pittsburgh 6, New York 5.   **First base on errors** — New York 3.

New York	ip	h	r	bb	k	**Pittsburgh**	ip	h	r	bb	k
Mathewson	8	7	2	2	1	Willis	8	6	2	1	1

Umpires — Messrs. Klem and Kane.   Attendance: 10,811 Time: 1:30

Game called in eighth, rain.

Bob Carroll's Pirate Legends

IN HIS 20 SEASONS (1910-29), CAREY STOLE 738 BASES WHILE LEADING THE N.L. IN STEALS 10 TIMES. IN 1922 HE WAS SUCCESSFUL ON 51 OF 53 ATTEMPTS!

A .285 CAREER HITTER, CAREY'S BEST SEASON WITH A BAT WAS 1925 WHEN HE WAS 35. HE BATTED .343, THEN HIT .458 IN THE WORLD SERIES DESPITE A CRACKED RIB.

Max **CAREY**

WAS ONE OF THE BEST CENTERFIELDERS IN NATIONAL LEAGUE HISTORY, AS WELL AS A RELIABLE LEADOFF HITTER AND SUPERB BASE STEALER.

CLARKE'S 506 STOLEN BASES HELPED HIM SCORE 1,619 RUNS.

AS PITTSBURGH'S MANAGER, HE TOOK HIS TEAM TO PENNANTS IN 1901-02-03 & TO A WORLD CHAMPIONSHIP IN 1909.

Fred **CLARKE**

WENT 5-FOR-5 IN HIS FIRST MAJOR LEAGUE GAME AND WENT ON TO POST A .312 BATTING AVERAGE OVER 21 SEASONS (1894-1915).

CUYLER WON GAME TWO OF THE 1925 WORLD SERIES WITH A HOMER, THEN DOUBLED OFF WALTER JOHNSON WITH THE BASES LOADED TO WIN GAME SEVEN FOR THE PIRATES.

Kiki **CUYLER**

HIT OVER .350 FOUR TIMES & FINISHED HIS 18-SEASON CAREER (1921-38) WITH A MARK OF .321. A SPEEDY & GRACEFUL OUTFIELDER, CUYLER PLAYED ON 4 PENNANT-WINNERS.

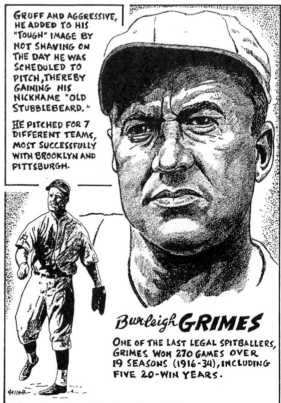

GRUFF AND AGGRESSIVE, HE ADDED TO HIS "TOUGH" IMAGE BY NOT SHAVING ON THE DAY HE WAS SCHEDULED TO PITCH, THEREBY GAINING HIS NICKNAME "OLD STUBBLEBEARD."

HE PITCHED FOR 7 DIFFERENT TEAMS, MOST SUCCESSFULLY WITH BROOKLYN AND PITTSBURGH.

Burleigh **GRIMES**

ONE OF THE LAST LEGAL SPITBALLERS, GRIMES WON 270 GAMES OVER 19 SEASONS (1916-34), INCLUDING FIVE 20-WIN YEARS.

Yellowhorse the Pirate

A proud man, who despite a short career, was a hero to his people

By William Jakub

PITTSBURGH BASEBALL has been blessed with its share of giants: from those who made their fame here as players, coaches, managers, or front office personnel to those who passed through before or after making their names elsewhere. But just a notch below the heroes in the pantheon are a number of lesser-gifted athletes who in their own enigmatic way contributed to baseball lore.

One such athlete was Moses "Chief" Yellowhorse. His primary claim to fame was his heritage. Moses Yellowhorse was a full-blooded Pawnee Indian. As one newspaper account of the time stated, "He was as dark as the previous night's lunar eclipse." As he strode to the mound, he was greeted by the wild beating of drums and war whoops from the adjacent grandstands. Regardless of whether he was home or away, Yellowhorse was met in this noisy fashion. Surprisingly, it never seemed to bother him or adversely affect his pitching. The fans loved doing it, and soon after Yellowhorse made his first appearance in a Pirate uniform (1921), he had become one of the town's favorite **native** sons.

During ballgames, whether the score

The Chief

was close or not, the familiar chant of "Put in Yellowhorse!" was resoundingly audible throughout the Bucs' Forbes Field. In fact, sometimes just the shouting of his name brought about the war whoops and drum tattoos. The tumultuous cacophony, reverberating through the ballyard, lent itself to a carnival atmosphere. Yellowhorse was truly a fan favorite, a man of the people.

He had arrived in the Steel City by way of Arkansas. Pirate President/Owner Barney Dreyfuss, known for his keen eye in judging baseball talent, believed Yellowhorse could help bring the Bucs back to their glory days. After its 1909 World's Championship (with the exception of the disaster years of 1914-17), the team had remained consistently over .500 and in the first division. For the Pirates it seemed to be "close, but no cigar," nearly every year.

During the 1921 and 1922 seasons, Yellowhorse was a sporadic contributor to the Pirate pitching staff. He finished his rookie season with a record of five wins and three losses, and sported a 2.98 ERA. He also became the only Pirate rookie pitcher to earn a victory on opening day. The Bucs took the Reds that day 8-7, and The Chief took the "W." Yellowhorse's second season as a Pirate was curtailed by illness and injury, limiting him to a 3-1 record and a 4.50 ERA. He did hit .316, though.

Although his overall record was nothing to brag about, he was fondly remembered. In later years his peers recounted that he threw as hard as Walter Johnson. Though not possessing a good curve, Yellowhorse compensated with velocity and accuracy, and a natural agility which made him a good fielder. His innate athletic ability and baseball savvy earned him accolades even from the likes of Commissioner Landis. The Judge earnestly believed that the young Yellowhorse was destined for baseball greatness. Unfortunately, his belief didn't come true.

In addition to injuries and illness, Yellowhorse's career was cut short by alcohol abuse, a plague which has bothered Native Americans in the bigs since Louis Sockalexis. When Yellowhorse returned to his tribe in Pawnee, Oklahoma, he was subject to a double-edged opinion of his reputation. On one hand, having been a major leaguer made him an object of esteem. Yet simultaneously, his tribe never forgave him for letting alcohol shorten his career.

Over time, the tribe began to accept him more openly. Between 1924 and the time of his death 40 years later, Yellowhorse tirelessly devoted his time and energy to promoting baseball among the young Pawnee. He was also very instrumental in revitalizing many of their lost traditions and language. He became a motivational factor in the lives of his people, especially the young. Yellowhorse's ability to perform, even under the most dire of circumstances, was largely attributed to the pride which he derived from his Pawnee heritage. His attempts to instill this pride and strength into his younger tribesmen did not go

unnoticed. In the eyes of the tribe, and especially the elders, he became one of their most beloved members. Tragically, he died of a sudden heart attack in 1964. He never married and fathered no children, yet he was survived by a legacy and a tribe that considered him both kindred spirit and favorite son.

From the 1930s into the late '50s, the spirit of The Chief still lived in Forbes Field. It is said that many Pirate fans of the time remember the cry of "Put in Yellowhorse!" starting, then abruptly dying away. Was the spirit of Yellowhorse still alive within the steel-girder superstructure of Forbes Field?

By the 1960s it was evident that the Pirates were destined to relocate to a new, yet familiar, locale. The move was largely caused by higher education sprawl, the whims of the then city fathers, and business entrepreneurs who believed they knew what was in the best interest of the populace.

As construction of the new facility began, the question was asked, "What shall this new colossus of a baseball home be called?" Some suggested "Allegheny Stadium," in honor of the river and the former city located on its banks. Others felt it should be named after a former Pirate great, such as Pie Traynor or "Flying Dutchman Field," after superstar Hans Wagner. A few pundits even offered the name of "Chief Yellowhorse Stadium," after the Bucco native American hurler of 50 years earlier.

Yellowhorse's easygoing demeanor won for him a place in the hearts of many Pittsburgh baseball fans. Although he possessed a keen awareness of the game and its intricacies, he was destined to be an average player at best. However, as a human being, he was a solid .300 hitter, lifetime. A Pittsburgh fan favorite, he became a solid citizen and hero to his tribespeople: both as a Pirate and a Pawnee, a class act.

Baseball Faces, Baseball Places

A photographic look at Pittsburgh and its region, from the collections of the Historical Society of Western Pennsylvania.

Presented by Corey Seeman

"Batter will be out," 1936. The Irene Kaufmann Settlement (IKS) was the primary settlement house for the Jewish population in Pittsburgh's Hill District. The IKS helped recent immigrants in Pittsburgh adapt to American life through numerous health and educational programs. The IKS was active in providing recreational activities, with baseball and basketball two of the most popular sports.

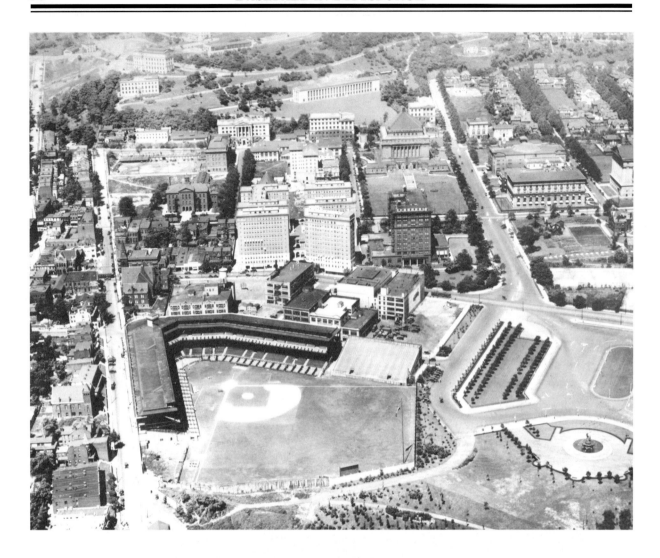

Opened during the 1909 season, Forbes Field was Pittsburgh's marquee stadium and home for sixty years. It was built in the Oakland neighborhood of Pittsburgh's East End and only a long fly ball away from Andrew Carnegie's greatest gifts to the city of Pittsburgh, the Carnegie Museum and the Carnegie Library of Pittsburgh. *Above,* aerial shot of Forbes Field, c1927. *Right,* Forbes Field press box, c1909.

A recent trend in ballpark design has mirrored an earlier era, the use of advertising signs on outfield walls. Forbes Field had such advertising only twice, encouraging fans to purchase War Bonds during World War I (*above*) and World War II. *Below*, Forbes entrance, c1950.

Opening Day marks the true beginning of Spring and people go to the ballpark not only to see a ballgame, but to be seen. In 1947, part-time Pirate owner and full-time entertainer Bing Crosby (*right*) greeted fans and Manager Billy Herman at Forbes Field. Long-time Pittsburgh Mayor David L. Lawrence throws out the first pitch, *below*. Lawrence was one of the driving forces behind the Pittsburgh "Renaissance," which modernized the City and helped remove the old "Smokey City" label. See postcard *opposite, bottom*.

Greatest flood ever recorded in Allegheny county, Mononaghela river guaging 36.2 ft. of water, and Allegheny river 36.6 ft. Next greatest flood, the celebrated "Pumpkin Flood" of 1832, followed by the 1884 flood, which was 3.3 ft. less.

Before Forbes Field, the Pirates played at Exposition Park, located on Pittsburgh's North Side in what is now the Three Rivers Stadium parking lot. The site was used for professional baseball since the 1880s. Despite its convenient location directly across the Allegheny River from downtown, Exposition Park was hardly ideal. The outfield was situated right on the river and often confronted outfielders with marshy conditions, forcing them to play out of position. Pittsburgh's Great Flood of 1907 (*above*) was no doubt sufficient incentive for the Pirates to move to Forbes Field, located high and dry in Oakland.

Scattered throughout the country were, (and continue to be) teams representing companies and communities, as well as groups of players who get together with little more than a love of the game. The teams pictured here are the Ambridge-Economy Baseball Team (*above*) from the adjacent communities northwest of Pittsburgh in Beaver County, and the Holy City team (*below left*), organized by the Metallurgical Chemistry Lab of Jones & Laughlin Steel Co. These teams would play at fields such as the West View Park Field (*below right*), part of the once-prominent entertainment complex in Pittsburgh's near North Hills.

Like the Holy City nine, the Scotch Bottom Team (*above*), was also linked to Jones & Laughlin. They rented a wagon from a livery stable for about $4 for a celebration near Expo Park for Pittsburgh's amateur teams, c1900. All classes and types of workers in Pittsburgh had teams. Here are the Asbestos Workers Team (*middle*), c1915. The Etna team (*bottom*) was a school or community team from the city north of Pittsburgh.

No matter who is playing, the World Series has long captured the attention of all baseball fans. Such was the case on October 16, 1911 (not August, as shown on photo) when the score of the Series game between the New York Giants and Philadelphia Athletics was posted outside Gus Miller's "Wonder Store" at the corner of Forbes and Oakland Avenues, just a block from Forbes Field's main entrance. The proprietor, Gus Miller, was nothing short of an Oakland neighborhood institution through his dual service as Forbes Field usher and owner of the best newsstand in the city. Miller opened his store in 1907, two years before the Pirates arrived in brand new Forbes Field. His choice of business was a natural considering the success he had as a newsboy, including the sale of 1200 copies of the Pittsburgh *Index* on October 24, 1906. Miller worked at his store every day until his death in 1967. Miller was an usher at Forbes from its 1909 opening through 1947. His birthday parties coincided with St. Patrick's Day and were an Oakland event, drawing many players and officials of the Pittsburgh Pirates and people from all across the city. Years after Miller's passing, the Pirates held a weekly luncheon for baseball fans — The "Gus Fan" Club.

Corey Seeman is head of reference and processing, Library and Archives Division, Historical Society of Western Pennsylvania, from whose files this photo section was compiled.

A Long Week of Homers

The stunning Dale Long achievement detailed — homer by homer

By Francis Kinlaw

DALE LONG, WHO APPEARED in over 1,000 major league games and tagged 132 big league home runs, is one of a select number of former Pittsburgh Pirates whose name elicits immediate recognition from those familiar with baseball's rich heritage. When he slammed home runs in eight consecutive games in May of 1956, the first baseman secured a special place in baseball history by establishing a remarkable record while facing intense pressure and unfavorable circumstances.

Until 1955, Long's career had been marked by a trail of frustrating and sometimes embarrassing experiences. After entering professional baseball in 1944, the fellow who came to be known to his Pittsburgh teammates as "The Big Guy" bounced all over the baseball horizon, playing for 15 teams in 11 leagues.

During that 11-year period, he was the property of six different major league organizations. But while the left-handed slugger had moved around the minors enough to be termed a "journeyman," he had by no means been mediocre. He had been the home run champion of two minor leagues, as well as the Most Valuable Player in the Pacific Coast League after his 35 homers and 135 RBIs helped bring the Hollywood Stars a pennant in 1953.

When Long finally landed in Pittsburgh in 1955, he immediately became an offensive star with 16 homers, 79 RBIs, and a .291 batting average.

He might have reached the fences more often had he not played so many of his 131 games in expansive Forbes Field. But the existence of that park's deep power alleys did enable him to rip 13 triples—enough to tie Willie Mays for the National League lead in that category. (Those three-baggers did **not** result from Long's speed or daring baserunning: the 6'4", 215-pounder did not steal a single base during the 1955 season!) Despite his contributions, however, the Pirates were mired in an era of futility, finishing in last place for the fourth consecutive year and deep in the National League's second division for the ninth time in 10 seasons since the end of World War II.

Both the career of the 30-year-old Long and the fortunes of the Pirates seemed to gain new life in the first month of the 1956 season, with Long's name often appearing in headlines above accounts of Pittsburgh victories. Exhibiting "high school enthusiasm," the young Pittsburgh club carried a respectable 12-12 record into a game with the Cubs on Saturday, May 19. Long, who was hitting .388 with six home runs and 18 RBIs, had not been the only productive Pittsburgh player. Shortstop Dick Groat, outfielders Frank Thomas and Gene Freese, and catcher Hank Foiles were also enjoying early success. Pitchers Bob Friend, Vernon Law and Ron

Kline were impressive as they assumed most of the mound duties.

On May 19, the most exciting week of the Pirate season — and of Dale Long's career — began in Forbes Field. Pittsburgh held a 5-3 lead in the bottom of the eighth inning when Long, who had already registered two RBIs with a double, homered off lefthander Jim Davis with one man on. After a mild Chicago rally was subdued in the ninth, the Bucs celebrated their 7-4 victory and advancement into fifth place, only three games behind the league-leading Milwaukee Braves.

The Pirates had an excellent opportunity to gain ground on the Braves the next day in a doubleheader with Milwaukee at Forbes Field. Brave righthander Ray Crone carried a 1-0 lead into the bottom of the fifth inning of the opener. But Long uncorked a three-run blast into the upper deck in right field to key a six-run uprising that carried the Pirates to victory. The crowd of 32,346 — the largest gathering in Forbes Field in five years — was to derive additional joy from the nightcap of the twin bill.

With Roberto Clemente on base in the bottom of the first inning, Long jumped on an offering from high-kicking southpaw Warren Spahn and promptly put the Pirates ahead by two runs. Long also singled across a pair of runs in the seventh inning, but Ron Kline hardly needed the insurance as he checked the Braves until a 5-0 Pittsburgh win was in the books.

Following a day off, Long launched his 10th home run of the season — and the fourth of his streak — against the St. Louis Cardinals on Tuesday night, May 22. With the Pirates trailing 3-1 and no one on base in the bottom of the sixth inning, Long connected with a delivery from righthander Herm Wehmeier so solidly that the ball ricocheted off a girder in the second tier of Forbes Field's right-field stands. Stan Musial, a veteran of 14 National League seasons, commented that he had never seen a ball hit so far in Pittsburgh. For the Bucs, however, the home run was the highlight of the evening, as the Cardinals handed the local team its lone defeat of this incredible week.

Long performed another Mickey Mantle imitation the next night, depositing a seventh-inning pitch by Card Lindy McDaniel over the 436-foot marker in right-center field. The tape-measure shot was reportedly the first batted ball to clear that distant spot in Forbes Field's 47 years. The home run produced the final run in a 6-0 Pirate victory but it possessed a drama of its own. Not only was the wallop compared to the 714th of Babe Ruth's career — which flew over the right-field roof in 1935 — but Long tagged this one in his fourth (and last) at bat of the evening.

This smash, despite its relative insignificance in the context of the game, brought loud cheers from the crowd of 19,917. For the second consecutive evening, attendance in Forbes Field was greater than it had been for any night game in four years, since June 6, 1952. Attention was focusing on the streak. Long later admitted that he was affected by the changing environment, saying that he had been "feeling loose" until he extended his home-run streak to five games with the homer off McDaniel.

Two days later, Long went deep against left-hander Curt Simmons in Philadelphia. The Pirates trailed the Phillies 3-2 in the fifth inning, and had Lee Walls aboard after drawing a base on balls, when Long rifled the blow that propelled Pittsburgh to an 8-5 triumph.

By homering in six straight contests, Long equaled a major league mark which had been reached by five men (Ken Williams in 1922, Long George Kelly in 1924, Lou Gehrig in 1931, Walker Cooper in 1947, and Willie Mays in 1955). But celebrity status came with a price. Long, a former semipro football star who had wandered for years through the baseball desert, would recall afterward that the hustle and bustle around him became a distraction after he had tied the existing record. Subtle pressure was applied, for example, when photographers asked Long to pose during the following day's batting practice with

to settle for a double. He then hit a high fly to centerfield in the third inning, and lined sharply to right in the fifth.

Long had one more opportunity to keep his streak alive. With the bases empty

A crowd of delighted fellow Bucs greet Long as he heads home
after slugging a homer in a seventh consecutive game.

seven of his 35-inch, 34-ounce bats "just in case he hit a homer in a seventh consecutive game."

And he tried to do exactly that by aiming for the fences of Connie Mack Stadium with every swing of the bat on Saturday afternoon, May 26. The suspense was almost lifted in the first inning when Long faced righthander Stu Miller and belted a drive that struck a spot less than one foot below the top of the 32-foot right-field wall. He was forced

and the Pirates holding a 4-2 lead in the eighth inning, he came to the plate to face righthander Ben Flowers. The count progressed to two balls and two strikes, the latter resulting when Long took two big swings but missed. ("He looked terrible!" said Pittsburgh manager Bobby Bragan.) Then, suddenly, came the record-breaker, as Long timed a knuckleball perfectly and knocked it over the light tower in right field and onto the porch of a neighboring house. Long's excited teammates bolted from their first-base dugout as soon as the ball was hit, mobbed him as he crossed home plate, and carried him to the dugout to the sound of applause from the sparse gathering of 4,614 Philadelphia fans. Frank Thomas, the next batter, then capped the celebration and ended the day's scoring by cracking a home run into the upper deck behind left field.

Rain caused postponement of a scheduled Sunday doubleheader against the Phillies, but the Sabbath brought no rest for baseball's latest sensation. Deals were negotiated with companies on both sides of the health spectrum: Long endorsed not only a bakery and a dairy, but also a brewery and Viceroy cigarettes. A "Dale Long T-shirt" was rushed onto the market and an appearance on "The Ed Sullivan Show" was arranged. And, with much fanfare, Pirates General Manager Joe L. Brown increased Long's salary from $13,500 to $15,700. All of these developments were unprecedented for a man who had struggled, as broadcaster Bob Prince once noted, "to get his name in a box score."

When the Pirates returned to Forbes Field on the evening of May 28 to begin a series with the Brooklyn Dodgers, they were greeted by an enthusiastic throng of 32,221. Long was challenged by Carl Erskine, a pitcher with a splendid overhand curve ball, and the veteran hurler ruled in the initial confrontation by enticing Long — who was again batting third — to ground out.

But after the Dodgers had taken a 2-1 lead, Long led off the bottom of the fourth inning by stroking one of Erskine's notorious low curves into the lower right-field stands, just above the 375 marker.

Bob Prince called the scene his "most significant moment in broadcasting." The cheers from the crowd had begun when Long stepped into the batter's box to hit, and ended several minutes later when he reluctantly popped out of the dugout to doff his cap and wave. (While commonplace today, such a response was extraordinary at the time: Branch Rickey said that Long's curtain call was the first one he had ever observed on a baseball field.) The game itself came to a halt as home plate umpire Lee Ballanfant called for a pause until the volume of noise lessened.

Though Long fanned in his last two plate appearances of the evening, the Pirates pushed one more run across for a 3-2 win. The local favorites had closed to within a single game of first place and continued to amaze nearly every so-called expert.

But the exhausting week was taking its toll on the team's offensive leader. Though he needed rest to prepare for another game with the Dodgers the next afternoon (May 29), Long was unable to sleep until 2:30 A.M.. Less than two hours later he was awakened by a telephone solicitation to appear on the "Today Show" that very morning. At 7:00 A..M. he lumbered out of bed and headed to a Pittsburgh studio for the television interview. Then he ate breakfast and drove to Forbes Field to face hard-throwing Don Newcombe, who would win 27 games during the season and receive both the National League Most Valuable Player Award and the major leagues' first Cy Young Award.

As Long kept his appointment with Newcombe, Senator James H. Duff of Pennsylvania was calling the attention of Congress to the eight-game streak. Unfortunately, at the ballpark, the Pirates and their star were experiencing an afternoon which did not match the sunny sky overhead. As the Dodgers rolled to a 10-1 victory, Long struck out on five pitches in the opening frame, flew to deep center in the third, and popped out in the sixth and eighth innings.

He did quicken the hearts of the 11,935 paying customers with his third-inning smash — Duke Snider was forced to make a running catch just in front of the ivy-covered outfield wall. But Forbes Field's unforgiving dimensions and an undeniable fatigue factor combined to bring the streak to an end. Long would contend that newspaper reporters were mistaken when they wrote after the game that Newcombe had overpowered him. Long said that he was simply too tired to get his bat around on a fireballer of Newk's quality.

In the eight games in which he had homered, Long had produced 19 runs and hit at a .500 clip (15 for 30). But just two weeks after the binge, Long fouled consecutive pitches off the same ankle, and his success hit the skids. The publicity of his streak had been so great that he received more votes for a position on the National League All-Star team than any other player. But he was in the midst of a deep slump when the game took place. After hitting 14 homers in the Pirates' first 33 games, Long tagged only 13 more over the remainder of the season.

The Pirates' fortunes followed suit. In second place with a proud 19-13 record on the last day of Long's streak, the club fell off the ledge and landed in seventh place with a 66-88 tally, a full 27 games short of the pennant.

Why was Long's streak so fascinating to baseball fans in 1956, and why is it still remembered fondly 39 years later? First and foremost, the pressure Long encountered and mastered demands appreciation. Second, the big first sacker was an appealing character because he was not a major star of whom great achievement was expected. Third, though the Pirates were planting the first seeds of their 1960 world championship, Long's team was so identified with failure that a popular movie of the period, *Angels in the Outfield*, had exploited the club's futility. And finally, the streak is noteworthy because Long victimized three of baseball's best pitchers (Spahn, Simmons and Erskine) during the memorable week.

By the time Don Mattingly and Ken Griffey, Jr. matched Long's feat, both those well-known players had tasted success and had appeared on the covers of numerous magazines. The relatively obscure Long, in contrast, had sparked the imagination of fans and gained much of his fame in only a few days. When Dale Long died of cancer in January of 1991, a large measure of that fame endured, and it will as long as baseball's great stories are told.

Tales from the Cheap Seats: Lew Burdette

Just like in the movies. I'm sitting at one end of the bar, nursing a diet ginger ale, hoping to see some old ballplayers. They are staying at the hotel for the Old Timers' Game.

"Who's the old gentleman sitting over there?" I ask the bartender.

"Why, that's Lew Burdette," he says.

Lew Burdette. Nitro, West Virginia. 203 career wins. My heart stops. Or maybe it's shrinking to the size it was when I was nine years old and Lew Burdette was beating the Yankees three times in the '57 World Series.

"Pour Mr. Burdette a drink for me and put it on my tab."

The bartender goes over and whispers in his ear. Lew Burdette looks up, smiles,and waves at me to come on over. I smile back and wave. God, I wasn't this suave trying to pick up girls when I was single. With Lew Burdette, I'm Charles Boyer. I should be wearing a tuxedo. The piano should be playing "As Time Goes By." The whole scene should be in black and white.

I walk over, introduce myself and sit down. An hour later I know how to throw a spitball, how to make it look like you're throwing a spitball when you're not, how to pitch to Willie Mays, and how Orlando Cepeda can't hit if you tell him what's coming. All very useful information.

I'm also sloshed. Burdette is fine.

See ya, Lew. Oh yeah, my kid says thanks for the autograph.

And Mom said nothing good can come from hanging around in bars.

Dr. Howard Elson

(From Dr. Elson's commentaries on KDKA Radio.)

AlphaBuc Soup

Versifying some great Pirate memories

By Gene "Two-Finger" Carney

Copyright 1991 by Gene Carney

A is for Adams
The Babe in '09
Won three Series games —
He knew when to shine.

B is for Bierbauer
"Pirated" away,
Mace Brown, Blass & Burgess:
Killer B's of their day.

C is for Candy
And Camnitz and Cooper
And for proud Clemente
Roberto was Super.

D is for Dreyfuss
Our great owner, Barney
And also for Danny,
That's Murtaugh, as in blarney!

E is for Ellis
The redoubtable Dock
When he took the mound
He made the game rock!

F is for Friend
Bob the right-handed ace
And F also stands
For the Fireman, Roy Face.

G is for Greenberg
Big Hank and his Gardens;
To skip Groat and Garms
Would deserve no pardons.

H is for Hot Corner:
Don Hoak and Rich Hebner
And for Harvey Haddix
Whose gem we'll long treasure.

I's for Impossible
The Pirate teams that
Were Battling Bucs
To their final at-bat.

J is for Jake
Beckley, Old Eagle Eye
And J is for Joe Brown
GM and great guy.

K is for Kiner
Ralph was our top gun
When he came to bat
He made Aunt Minnie run!

L is for Long
We cheered Dale's eight dingers
And for Vernon Law
The Deacon threw zingers.

M is for Maz
Whose play did transcend
And for Meyer and Mizell
Of Vinegar Bend.

N is for Nelson
Our Rocky, and Klu
First base was their domain
With E-3 slugger Stu.

O is for Oliver
Scoop sure swung the Lumber
He did it with Company
They could hit in their slumber.

P is for Phillippe
An earlier Deacon
And for Gunner Prince
Whose voice was a beacon.

Q is for Quality
The Waners had tons
Big Poison and Little
Turned hits into runs.

R is for Rowswell
A Rosey is a Rosey
And R is for Robertson
Bob's clouts made leads cozy

S is for Stargell
That wonderful Will
And for Sewell whose eephus pitch
Blooped from the hill.

T is for Pie
The gentleman Traynor
Class, grace and style
Never seen plainer.

U's for United
As in U.S.A.
Whose anthem we sing
Before we start play.

V is for Vaughan
Arky's .385
Is tops for all Buccos
Long gone or alive.

W is for Wagner
Honus rated the Hall
For hitting and stealing
And fielding the ball.

X is for Max
(Just turn it around)
Carey was as fleet
As any greyhound.

You must realize
Not all Bucs can be fitted
And forgiveness, please,
For those names omitted.

Z is for Zillions
The number of cheers
Our Pirates have earned
By their feats o'er the years.

Bob Carroll's Pirate Legends

GROAT JUMPED STRAIGHT FROM THE DUKE CAMPUS TO THE PITTSBURGH PIRATES IN 1952.

HE WAS N.L. MVP IN 1960 WHEN HE LED THE PIRATES TO A WORLD TITLE WITH A LEAGUE-BEST .325 BATTING AVERAGE. IN 1964, HE HELPED THE CARDINALS WIN A WORLD CHAMPIONSHIP.

Dick GROAT

WAS AN OUTSTANDING ATHLETE — AN ALL-AMERICA BASKETBALL STAR AT DUKE, TWO YEARS STARRING IN PRO BASKETBALL, AND 14 SEASONS AS A TOP MAJOR LEAGUE SHORTSTOP.

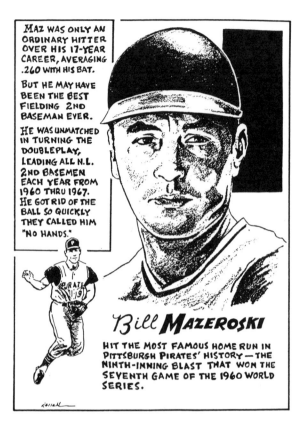

MAZ WAS ONLY AN ORDINARY HITTER OVER HIS 17-YEAR CAREER, AVERAGING .260 WITH HIS BAT.

BUT HE MAY HAVE BEEN THE BEST FIELDING 2ND BASEMAN EVER.

HE WAS UNMATCHED IN TURNING THE DOUBLEPLAY, LEADING ALL N.L. 2ND BASEMEN EACH YEAR FROM 1960 THRU 1967. HE GOT RID OF THE BALL SO QUICKLY THEY CALLED HIM "NO HANDS."

Bill MAZEROSKI

HIT THE MOST FAMOUS HOME RUN IN PITTSBURGH PIRATES' HISTORY — THE NINTH-INNING BLAST THAT WON THE SEVENTH GAME OF THE 1960 WORLD SERIES.

NO THIRDSACKER WAS BETTER AT GOING TO HIS RIGHT.

SPORTSWRITERS ROUTINELY WROTE THAT AN OPPONENT "DOUBLED DOWN THE THIRD BASE LINE, BUT TRAYNOR THREW HIM OUT!"

Pie TRAYNOR

WAS "MR. THIRDBASE" IN HIS DAY (1920-37), A CAREER .320 HITTER WHO WAS MORE FAMOUS FOR HIS GLOVE THAN HIS BAT.

A SLASHING, LINE-DRIVE HITTER, "BIG POISON" HAD ONLY 113 HOMERS BUT HIS 603 DOUBLES AND 190 TRIPLES LED TO 1,309 RBI AND 1,626 RUNS SCORED.

HIS HITTING WAS GREAT DESPITE HIS WELL-KNOWN TASTE FOR NIGHTLIFE. ONCE HE WENT ON THE WAGON, BUT WHEN HE SLUMPED AT BAT HIS MANAGER ORDERED HIM TO THE NEAREST BAR.

Paul WANER

AVERAGED .333 OVER HIS 20-YEAR CAREER (1926-45) AND COLLECTED 3,152 BASE HITS.

The Pennsylvania State Association, 1934-1942

The struggle to keep minor league baseball alive in western Pennsylvania

By Corey Seeman

MINOR LEAGUE BASEBALL has enjoyed great success in western Pennsylvania from the earliest days of professional baseball through the 1950s. Leagues such as the Iron and Oil League, Western Pennsylvania Association, Ohio-Pennsylvania League, and others operated in the region. While many of these leagues came and went, the two most prominent minor leagues to play here were the Middle Atlantic League (1925-1951) and the Pennsylvania State Association (1934-1942). Both were particularly blessed to have been led by Elmer Daily of Ebensburg, Pa., who brought professional baseball to people all over western Pennsylvania.

The Middle Atlantic League had teams in almost all of the region's cities including Wheeling, West Virginia; Youngstown, Akron, and Canton, Ohio; Cumberland, Maryland; and western Pennsylvania cities such as Altoona, Johnstown, Erie, New Castle, and others. In addition, the Middle Atlantic League had a unqiue farm league, the Class D Pennsylvania State Association, that operated from 1934 to 1942. During the Great Depression, the Middle Atlantic League remained viable, but was left with few teams from western Pennsylvania. The league that boasted four of the eight teams from western Pennsylvania in 1930 (Charleroi, Jeannette, Johnstown and Scottdale), only had Johnstown from the region in 1933. Middle Atlantic

League President Daily and Secretary-Treasurer Russell Hockenbury (Scottdale, Pa.), who were both from the region, saw the creation of the Pennsylvania State Association as a solution to two problems.

The Pennsylvania State Association was formed in 1934 with six teams, all located less than fifty miles from Pittsburgh. The six original teams included Jeannette and Greensburg in Westmoreland County; Charleroi, Monessen and McKeesport along the Monongahela River to the east and south; and Washington, Pennsylvania. According to the history of the Middle Atlantic League, Daily "...conceived the idea of a closely knit circuit whereby the teams could travel to distant towns and back to its [sic] home port the same night," thus dramatically reducing operating expenses. Most of these cities grew on the backs of varied industry in the region including steel, glass, coal and coke.

The closest league city to Pittsburgh was McKeesport, the home to nearly 55,000 people and the huge steel mills of American Sheet and Tin Plate Company and the National Tube Company of National Steel. Charleroi was a city of just over 10,000 and a center for glass production and coal mining on the Monongahela River. Charleroi was also the home of National League President and Pennsylvania Governor John Tener. Monessen was the classic industrial boomtown and was founded in 1898. By 1940, the population was just over 20,000, with a great deal of its work force employed at either American Sheet and Tin Plate Company or Pittsburgh Steel.

In Westmoreland County, Jeannette (population 15,126) and county seat Greensburg (population 16,508), were industrial and coal-mining centers with factories producing machinery, glass, and plumbing supplies Washington (population 24,545) is the county seat of Washington County, located south of Pittsburgh. Like other cities in the region, Washington's main industries were coal and glass and other natural resources including oil, clay, and limestone.

In the nine years that the Pennsylvania State Association operated, teams played in other regional cities including Beaver Falls, Butler, Johnstown, Oil City, and Warren, Ohio. Beaver Falls (population 17,000) is an industrial city located on the Beaver River near the Ohio River. Butler's population in 1930 was over 23,000 and was the home of the Pullman-Standard railroad car company and ARMCO. Oil City (population 22,075) was a major oil center located on the Allegheny River north of Pittsburgh. Although western Pennsylvania was no longer the center of the national petroleum industry in the 1940s as it had been in the 19th century, businesses in the city still were prominently connected with the oil industry.

Located in Cambria County to the east of Pittsburgh, Johnstown is one of the largest industrial cities outside the Monongahela and Ohio River valleys and the home of the Cambria Plant of Bethlehem Steel. With a population of 66,610 in 1940, Johnstown was the largest city to participate in the Pennsylvania State Association. Games played in Johnstown were at Point Stadium, located at the confluence of the Little Conemaugh and Stony Creek Rivers.

Many Pennsylvania State Association players went on to major league careers, with a few attaining great prominence. Possibly the greatest player in the Association was Monessen's 1934 all-star centerfielder Tommy Henrich, later one of the stars of the New York Yankee championship nines. Henrich played his second professional season in the Middle Atlantic League for the Zanesville Greys and hit .337. Another great was Butler Yankees first baseman Hank Sauer, who in his second season in the league, led the Association with a .351 batting average. Born in Pittsburgh in 1919, Sauer played the 1939 season for the Akron club of the MAL before playing for the Reds, Cubs, Cardinals and Giants. Other players who graduated from the Pennsylvania State Association to the major leagues include: Harry Craft, Al Rubeling, Kenny Heintzelman, Mike McCormick, Joe Mack, Steve Souchock, and Joe Page.

For its first year, the Pennsylvania State Association adopted a split-season, with a season-ending playoff. The Association played all day games. In 1934, Greensburg, winner of the second half, defeated Washington, winner of the first half, four games to two, to claim the first league title. While its initial season was generally a success, the Association suffered its first casualty afterward when the Jeannette franchise was replaced by Butler.

Butler became the most successful club in the Association, winning five championships in eight years. The Butler franchise also was consistently among the leaders in attendance. Monessen defeated Washington in the 1935 playoffs. For the 1936 season, Jeannette returned to the league as a Pittsburgh Pirate affiliate, replacing the Washington franchise that was unable to find a suitable stadium in which to play. In 1936, Charleroi also left the Association and was replaced by Beaver Falls. The neighboring cities Jeannette and Greensburg won the first- and second-half titles respectively, with Jeannette winning the playoffs.

The 1937 season was the most trying in the Association's history. The season opened with cold and rainy weather that forced teams to cancel numerous games. Furthermore, western Pennsylvania cities were particularly hard hit during the Depression year of 1937 as factories routinely closed or cut back the workforce. The financially weakened six-club league finally opened on May 13, but within one month, two clubs shut their gates Both McKeesport and 1936 champs Jeannette folded on June 10 and were not replaced, leaving the league with four teams. At that time, the Butler Yankees were well in front with a 19-4 record. Jack Dunlevy, president of the Butler club, offered to restart the season, allowing the remaining three teams a fair chance at catching the Yankees. The "new" season was also split, half running from June 11 to July 20 and the second half from July 21 to August 29. Butler still won the first half crown and took the playoffs four games to three over Beaver Falls.

To curb declining attendance, lights were installed in the Greensburg and Butler ballparks in 1937 The Association continued as a four-club league in 1938 with Monessen being replaced by McKeesport, a club that had folded one month into the previous season. Despite being affiliated with the Pittsburgh Pirates, the McKeesport Little Pirates almost did not start the year, citing many of the same economic problems that had caused them to fold in '37. Early 1938 was also plagued by inclement weather, causing the cancellation of the first two days of the season. Butler eventually won their second straight championship, defeating McKeesport, four games to one.

In 1939 the Pennsylvania State Association returned as a six-club league. Washington rejoined the association and a team was placed in Johnstown to replace a Middle Atlantic League club that had moved to Youngstown, Ohio. The Johnstown franchise was supported by the community group, the Johnnies, that sought to keep professional baseball in Johnstown. This group was later instrumental in getting a franchise in the Middle Atlantic League after World War II. For 1939 , the league changed their format to incorporate Shaughnessy playoffs for the top four teams in the six-club league. Washington defeated Butler three games to none to win the championship.

Problems in the Pennsylvania State Association continued in 1940 .Before the season opener, charter club Greensburg was transferred to Warren, a city in eastern Ohio. As in 1937, bad weather conditions early in the '40 season presented many problems for league president Daily. That year's recap in *The Sporting News Baseball Guide* stated that "...it took all of President Daily's long experience and thorough acquaintance with conditions to keep things going — or even get started."

The volatile franchise in McKeesport folded for the second time on July 5, 1940 and was moved to Oil City, Pennsylvania. With the support of the local newspaper, the *Oil City Blizzard*, residents staged a "whirlwind campaign to obtain the franchise," and the publisher of the *Blizzard* guaranteed any shortage for the financing of the team. Butler continued their winning ways by downing Beaver Falls in the 1940 playoffs, three games to none.

1941 opened with the same six teams and ended with Butler taking the Shaughnessy playoffs over Washington. The only stadium not lit by this time was Johnstown's Point Stadium. Warren and Beaver Falls failed to open the 1942 season, leaving the league once again with just four teams — The Butler Yankees, Johnstown Johnnies, Oil City Oilers, and Washington Red Birds.It was the Pennsylvania State Association's last season in 1942 and it ended as most of the others had, with the Butler Yankees as the champion. The Yankees were the Association champions in five of the last six years of the league. The sole team to prevent them from landing six straight titles were the Washington Red Birds, victors over Butler in the 1939 playoffs.

Like most minor leagues at the end of the 1942 season, the Pennsylvania State Association ceased operations in 1943 for the duration of World War II. Baseball supporters in Butler held an annual "Community Baseball Bond Drive" from 1943 until 1945 and raised $175,000 each year for the war effort. While Daily and Hockenbury planned to commence play at the end of the war, the league never reorganized. However, many of the cities that hosted Pennsylvania State Association teams rejoined the Middle Atlantic League after the war including Butler, Johnstown, and Oil City. The presence of Pennsylvania State Association teams keeping their communities interested in professional baseball made possible the placement of numerous western Pennsylvania teams in the Middle Atlantic League after the war. With the exception of Erie, Pa.,in the New York-Penn League and Johnstown in the independent Frontier League, minor league baseball has all but disappeared in this region since the mid-1950s. Still, the legacy of minor league baseball in the region should be greatly attributed to the work of Elmer Daily and the presence of the Pennsylvania State Association.

PHOTO CREDITS

Pages 4, 6, 7, 9, 13, 14, 39, 63 — Pittsburgh Pirates.
Pages 29, 30, 31, 32, 33, 34, 35, 36, 58 — Historical Society of Western Pennsylvania.
Page 27 — Bill Jakub

The Pittsburgh Keystones and the 1887 Colored League

A Radical New Concept in Team Ownership

By Jerry Malloy

[A note of thanks for research compiled by Raymond J. Nemec, Vern Luse, L. Robert Davids, and Robert W. Peterson.— J.M.]

ALTHOUGH PHILADELPHIA WAS The most prominent center of early African-American baseball, the 1887 Pittsburgh Keystones produced the leadership for the era's most successful (or, least unsuccessful) black baseball league, the League of Colored Base Ball Clubs.

Commonly referred to as the "Colored League" or the "National Colored League," it barely managed to get off the ground and crashed prematurely, providing a paltry precursor to the Negro National League which Rube Foster would found 33 years later, in 1920. Yet the ill-starred circuit's contribution to the history of black baseball, and Pittsburgh's role in it, is worth noting. For, not only did the Colored League launch several notable careers, most significantly that of the Keystones' Sol White, it also accomplished something that even the formidable Foster could barely even hope to dream: it was accepted, if not exactly embraced, by the exalted polity of Organized Baseball's National Agreement.

On the Same Footing As Whites

The prospect of organizing this league meets with the hearty approval of every person as something that should have been done long ago, so that our people could have been on the same footing as whites so far as baseball is concerned.
Walter S. Brown, *Sporting Life*, October 27, 1886.

The Colored League was not the first known attempt to form a circuit of professional black teams. That distinction belongs to the Southern League of Colored Base Ballists of 1886, the subject of an article by Bill Plott in the *Baseball Research Journal* of 1974. Unfortunately, the historical record of this ambiguous enterprise remains etched in vapor. Individual statistics, team standings, and even league membership have eluded substantial recovery, as local press coverage was scattered and scant. Such was not the case with the black league of the following year. In October 1886, *Sporting Life* reported the intention of Walter S. Brown, owner of the Pittsburgh Keystones, to create a Colored League for 1887. Brown was a news agent at Pittsburgh's Central Hotel, as well as the Smoky City's correspondent for the *Cleveland Gazette*, a prominent African-American weekly newspaper.

Brown signaled his intention to muscle-up the local team by enlarging its name to the Big Keystone Base Ball Club. He also cast his net beyond the black neighborhoods of Pittsburgh, eventually signing two

Ohioans: Sol White, a slugging infielder from Bellaire, and catcher-outfielder Weldy Walker, of Steubenville, younger brother of Fleet Walker. Both Walkers had played for Toledo in 1884, when it was a member of the major league American Association, though Weldy's role was minor compared to Fleet's.

The upstart league received its first setback when the Cuban Giants, unwilling to sacrifice Sunday bookings in Brooklyn, New York, declined Brown's invitation to join. Based in Trenton, New Jersey, the Cuban Giants had just completed their inaugural season as the first team of salaried African-American ballplayers and already were established as the nation's most glamorous black team, a distinction it would retain throughout the 1880s. Indeed, Sol White, black baseball's first historian, wrote 20 years later that it had been the success of the Cuban Giants that "led some people to think that colored base ball, patterned after the National League ...would draw the same number of people."

Undeterred by the Giants' decision, Brown convened a December 9 meeting of delegates from Baltimore, Boston, Louisville, Philadelphia, Pittsburgh, and Washington, D.C., at Eureka Hall, on Pittsburgh's Arthur Street. Agents from Chicago failed to attend, but those from Cleveland and Cincinnati did. While neither city entered the league, Cincinnati was represented by Bud Fowler, the pioneering star black ballplayer and aspiring entrepreneur, who took time off from his winter job as a barber to investigate the Colored League's possibilities. The delegates elected Brown president, adopted the rules of Organized Baseball, and agreed to reconvene four months later in Baltimore where Brown would become league secretary.

In the meantime, league officials busied themselves with matters large and small. They spurned an offer from the Spalding Company to furnish a championship pennant in exchange for use of its baseballs. Instead they adopted the Reach ball, also used by the American Association, in return for providing awards (by various accounts, gold medals or trophies) for leaders in batting average and fielding percentage.

On March 14 and 15, 1887, delegates met at the Douglass Institute, a distinguished black social and cultural center in Baltimore. They acknowledged the experimental nature of the season by scheduling many open dates to allow for (hopefully) profitable exhibition games. Player salaries were to range from $10 to $75 per month; each club was to hire a local umpire; visiting teams were guaranteed $50 plus half the gate receipts ("the revenue from the grand stands not included"), and were to receive $25 from the home team in case of a rainout.

Just as future major league owners (especially in Pittsburgh and Washington, D.C.) would rent their stadiums to Negro League teams, two members of the Colored League, the Keystones and Lord Baltimores, arranged to play in major league parks: at Pittsburgh's National League grounds, Recreation Park, and at Oriole Park, home of the American Association's Baltimore team. The Falls City club of Louisville was said to be the only black team in the nation that owned its own grounds, "a handsome park at 16th Street and Magnolia avenue." However, construction of the park was not completed in time for the season opener on May 6.

In reporting that the players would average about $50 per month in salary, the *Cleveland Gazette* darkly asked, "Will they get their money?" But optimism reigned among the league's creators, who were "enthusiastic and say the success of the new organization is assured," wrote the *Gazette*. In a hearty spirit of self-congratulation, the delegates, in full evening attire, repaired to a lavish reception and banquet at the Douglass Institute, generously hosted by the Lord Baltimores.

Why Do They Need Protection?

The several minor [league] organizations that will form a combination against the League and American Association [includes]...the Colored League...
The Sporting News, January 15, 1887.

One source of this optimism was that the fledgling circuit had become party to the National Agreement, placing it within the orbit of what we now call Organized Baseball. On January 15, 1887, *TSN* published a roster of players signed by teams aligned with the National Agreement, including eight Colored League franchises: the Baltimore Lord Baltimores, Boston Resolutes, Cincinnati Browns, Louisville Falls City, New York Gorhams, Philadelphia Pythians, Pittsburgh Keystones, and Washington, D.C. Capital Citys. Neither Cincinnati nor Washington ever took the field, but the Capital Citys' proposed roster included Sol White and Frank C. Leland, both of whom would shape African-American baseball's destiny through the first decade of the next century. With the dawning of the new year, the new league was within the domain of Organized Baseball.

The Colored League joined an alliance of various minor leagues which was formed to combat the theft of players by the two major leagues. *Sporting Life* derided the Colored League's admission into baseball's official family as preposterous. "WHY DO THEY NEED PROTECTION,?" they bellowed on April 13th:

The League will attempt to secure the protection of the National Agreement. This can only be done with the consent of all the National Agreement clubs in whose territory the colored clubs are located. This consent should be obtainable, as these clubs can in no sense be considered rivals to the white clubs,

nor are they likely to hurt the latter in the least financially. Still[,] the League can get along without protection. The value of the latter to the white clubs lies in that it guarantees a club undisturbed possession of its players. There is not likely to be much of a scramble for colored players,...owing to the high standard of play required and to the popular prejudice against any considerable mixture of races.

In reality, the Colored League's desire to gain entry into organized baseball was far from fatuous. Rather, it was a pragmatic response to bitter experience. S.K. Govern, one of the Philadelphia Pythians' backers, had managed the Cuban Giants in 1886 (and would do so again in 1887). He undoubtedly reminded his colleagues that George Stovey, the masterful black pitcher, had been stolen from the Cuban Giants by the Eastern League's Jersey City team only six months prior, in mid-season. Without the protection of the National Agreement, the Cuban Giants were powerless to retain Stovey.

In addition, during the 1886 season, the Cuban Giant Arthur Thomas rejected an offer to sign with Philadelphia of the American Association, and Stovey nearly signed with the New York National League team. Even with the supposed protection of the National Agreement, there is evidence that white minor leagues were tampering with Colored League players as early as February 1887. Also, in 1887 African-Americans played on twelve minor league teams, seven of them for five clubs in the prestigious International League alone.

Not until 1889 did the mighty Cuban Giants join Organized Baseball, representing Trenton in the Middle States League. But the entire Colored League of 1887 could proclaim membership even before a game had been played.

The 13-Game Season

The National Colored League opened its championship season at Recreation Park, Pittsburgh, on May 6, in a game between the Gorhams of New York and the Keystones of Pittsburgh. Previous to the game there was a grand street parade and a brass band concert. The game was well contested and quite exciting. About twelve hundred people were present. The score was: Gorhams, 11; Keystones, 8.
The New York Freeman, May 14, 1887.

In February, *Sporting Life* predicted that it would be "highly improbable" that the Colored League would survive a single season, and they were emphatically correct. Appropriately, Pittsburgh, home of the league's flagship franchise, was the site of both the alpha and omega of its brief season. Thirteen days after the festive opener, the Keystones lost to the visiting Lord Baltimores, 6-2, in the last of the unlucky league's 13 games.

Before the Colored League was a week old, the Boston Resolutes were stranded in Louisville, reported *TSN*, and "at last accounts...were working their way home doing little turns in barbershops and waiting on table [sic] in hotels." The marooned Resolutes undoubtedly took small comfort in claiming the championship by winning their sole contest. By May 27, the Gorhams, Pythians, and Lord Baltimores were reported as "the only teams able to keep up," and one day later Walter Brown "reluctantly and sadly admitted that the Colored League was no more as an organization." The Colored League's final standings were as follows:

Wins Against

	Bo	Ph	NY	Pi	Ba	Lo	W-L	Pct.
Bos.	-	0	0	0	0	1	1-0	1.000
Phila.	0	-	1	1	2	0	4-1	.800
N.Y.	0	0	-	1	0	1	2-2	.500
Pgh	0	1	0	-	2	0	3-4	.428
Balt.	0	0	0	2	-	0	2-4	.333
Lou.	0	0	1	0	0	-	1-2	.333

Sol White attributed the league's quick demise to insufficient financial backing. Yet he had words of praise for the effort:

> [T]he short time of its existence served to bring out the fact that colored ball players of ability were numerous. The teams, with the exception of the Keystones, of Pittsburgh, and the Gorhams, of New York, were composed mostly of home talent, so they were not necessarily compelled to disband. With reputations as clubs from the defunct Colored League, they proved to be very good drawing cards in different sections of the country. The Keystones and Gorhams, especially distinguished themselves by later defeating the Cuban Giants.

Aftermath

The Colored League was the last hurrah in African-American baseball for the Pythians, though new owners attempted a reorganization. The Pythians were namesakes, rather than direct descendants, of the famed Philadelphia team whose application for membership in the National Association of Base Ball Players was rejected (in writing) in 1867, and was the first recorded black club to play a white team, two years later.

Black baseball's first backers were gentlemen's social clubs, such as the Pythians, but its future was in robust professionalism, with the Cuban Giants leading the way.

Among aspirants to their throne, the New York Gorhams gave the Cuban Giants their first stiff challenge. The Gorhams were run by player-manager Ambrose Davis, "the first colored man in the East to venture into professional baseball...," according to Sol White, who added that Davis "proved to be of great assistance to the game by his competitiveness in producing teams to combat the great Cuban Giants."

When the Colored League collapsed, Davis launched a tenacious campaign to supplant the Cuban Giants, culminating in 1891, when he signed most of their best players, and renamed his team the Big Gorhams. Sol White judged them the best team in 19th-century black baseball. Along the way, Davis doggedly continued to sign good players, even knowing that the best, such as Bob, Oscar, and Andy Jackson (the latter two brothers), and Sol White, would be gobbled up by the Cuban Giants. Other prominent Cuban Giants who had played in the Colored League were Arthur Thomas, William Selden, and William Malone.

The flagship team of the league, Brown's Pittsburgh Keystones, did not fare quite as well. They made one last run in 1888, when they finished second to the Cuban Giants — but ahead of Ambrose Davis' Gorhams — at a late-season tournament in Newburgh, New York. Davis retaliated by signing the Keystones' best player, Sol White. Thereafter, the Keystones may have carried on as a local semipro team. Sol White played briefly with the Keystones during a half-hearted attempt at a revival in 1892, but he quickly moved on.

As for Walter S. Brown, he was last seen in September 1888, sorting mail as a railroad postal clerk between Pittsburgh and New York City.

Tales from the Cheap Seats: The Wave

What is the surest sign of the decline of Western Civilization? Rampant drug abuse, disregard of the environment, the hypocrisy of our leaders? Maybe, but what ticks me off is the wave. Like the Pirates need an insurance run in what has been a great pitching duel. Ninth inning, man on second, nobody out, the most dramatic moment in the game. Everybody knows Lind is going to bunt to get Barry Bonds to third so a fly ball or a grounder not hit directly at a drawn-in infield will score the run. There's so much to watch it all can't be taken in at one time.

The pitcher trying to throw a high strike to make it harder to lay down a good bunt. The third baseman charging, shortstop breaking over, first baseman staying back, pitcher covering the first-base side. Or will the first baseman charge, second baseman cover and the third baseman stay back? Or will they decoy, or pitch out to make the runner commit too early and pick him off, or at least slow him up, concurrently seeing what the batter will do if he commits too early. This is exciting!

What's the crowd doing? Are they on the edge of their seats, anticipating the pitch? Are the arguing the merits of the different options?...Are they watching the game?

No. They are starting a wave.

Oh somewhere in this favored land, the sun is shining bright.
The band is playing somewhere, and somewhere hearts are light.
And baseball is exciting, the players strong and brave.
But Pittsburgh fans don't notice it. They're starting to do a wave.

Dr. Howard Elson

(From Dr. Elson's commentaries on KDKA Radio.)

Batting First for the Pirates in the 'Live Ball' Era

From CARSON to CARLOS

By Herman Krabbenhoft

Copyright 1995 by Herman Krabbenhoft

SOMEBODY HAS TO BAT FIRST — to help set the table for the sluggers in the heart of the lineup. And during the 75 years of the so-called "live ball" (i.e. since 1920), 35 different players have served as the principal leadoff batter for the Pirates in one or more seasons. This article takes a retrospective look at who they were and what some of them accomplished as first-up batters. A couple assembled outstanding records; and another was on the verge.

1920-1929
When the Elite Batted First

Carson Bigbee, an outfielder who spent his entire major league career (1916-1926) with the Bucs, was the first principal leadoff batter during the "live ball" era for Pittsburgh; he was their game starter nearly 85% of the time in the 1920 and 1921 campaigns (during which he put together an on base percentage of .348.)

Then a trio of eventual Hall of Famers took over the number-one slot in the batting order: Rabbit Maranville (1922 and 1923); Max Carey (1924-1926); and Lloyd "Little Poison" Waner (1927). Overall for the "Roaring Twenties" decade, Bigbee appeared in the most leadoff games with 326;

Maranville (who was a **Pirate** from 1921 through 1926) was next in line with 313 first-up games. For comparison, the NL's top leadoff batter (in terms of most leadoff games) in the 1920s was George Burns with 744 first-batter games.

1930-1939
The Senior Circuit's First Great Leadoff Batter in the "Live Ball" Era

After a phenomenal rookie season in 1927 (in which he fashioned a .355 batting average and a .390 on base percentage in 150 games — 132 as a leadoff batter), Lloyd Waner relinquished the role of principal first-up batter to Sparky Adams in 1928 and Dick Bartell in 1929. However, Waner reclaimed the primary slot in 1930 and held it for most of the decade. (Woody Jensen and Lee Handley handled primary leadoff duties for the 1936 and 1938 seasons, respectively.)

Unquestionably, Little Poison was the *numero uno* number-one batter in the National League during the noisy thirties. Overall, he appeared in 912 games as a leadoff batter (tops in the majors and 74% of all the games he played) and put together a .311 batting average and a .345 on base percentage.

Significantly, he became the first National Leaguer to surpass the 1000 lifetime leadoff games plateau; he finished his Big League career in 1945 with 1203 first-up contests — 1147 of them with the Pirates.

1940-1955
In Search of Another
Franchise Leadoff Batter (Part 1)

During the next 16 years, the Pirates had considerable difficulty coming up with a player who could handle the leadoff role on a year-to-year-to-year basis (as Little Poison had done). From 1940 through 1955, 10 different players tried to fulfill that obligation; none was successful — Lee Handley (1940 and 1946); Frankie Gustine and Alf Anderson (1941); Pete Coscarart (the War Years of 1942-1945); Billy Cox (1947); Stan Rojek (1948 and 1949); Bob Dillinger (1950); Pete Castiglione (1951); Clem Koshorek (1952); Cal Abrams (1953); Curt Roberts (1954); and even Roberto Clemente (1955, his rookie year, and 1957).

1956-1970
Some Stability at the Top

In 1956 (following four consecutive cellar finishes), the Bucs finally acquired a leadoff batter who would help them climb ultimately to the top of the diamond world in 1960. That May, Bill Virdon, the 1955 NL Rookie of the Year, was obtained from the Cardinals for pitcher Dick Littlefield and hometown hero, outfielder Bobby Del Greco. While Virdon didn't make people forget Little Poison, he did stabilize the top of the Pirate batting order, serving as their principal leadoff batter for six years (1956 and 1958-1962). By the time he retired after the 1965 campaign, he had amassed a total of 634 first-up games, the second highest total in Pirate history during the "live ball" era. During his principal leadoff years he compiled a .264 batting average and a

.318 on base percentage.

Dick Schofield took over as the primary first-up for the Corsairs for the 1963 and 1964 seasons. And Bonus Baby Bob Bailey had that responsibility in 1965. Then, for 1966, Pittsburgh obtained Matty Alou from San Francisco and inserted him at the top of the order for 122 games. Under the fast-talking tutelage of Buc Skipper Harry Walker (translated deftly by Roberto Clemente), the diminutive Dominican outfielder responded with a league-leading .342 batting average. He thus became only the second principal leadoff batter in the NL (during the "live ball" era) to capture a batting crown. New Hall-of-Famer Richie Ashburn of the cross-state Philadelphia Phillies had been the first one to achieve the feat. And he did it twice.

In spite of Alou's outstanding hitting ability, the Pirates brought in an established leadoff batter to share the first-up duties with him in the next campaign. In 1967, Alou led off 81 games in which he batted a nifty .324 (.338 overall), while Maury Wills, a six-time stolen base champion, led off 79 games, in which he batted an even .300. And in 1968, Wills took over as primary leadoff guy, sporting a .289 mark in 118 games, while Alou was a backup leadoff batter, hitting .337 in 20 games there.

Then, with Wills gone in the expansion draft, Alou returned to the number-one slot full-time in 1969, appearing first up in 161 games and putting together a glowing .331 batting average and a .371 on base percentage. He remained the Pirate principal leadoff batter in 1970 (115 games) although his overall batting average dropped to .297. Following the 1970 campaign, Alou was dealt to the Cards, thus ending a period of stability at the top of the order for Pittsburgh.

Overall, Matty Alou had appeared in 499 games as a Bucco leadoff batter. During his five years in Pittsburgh, he compiled a very impressive .327 batting average and a

.358 on base percentage — numbers in line with those carved out by the legendary Lloyd Waner.

1971-1985
In Search of Another
Franchise Leadoff Batter (Part 2)

Following Alou's departure, the Pirates employed four different players as their principal leadoff batters during the next eight seasons. Dave Cash was the man in 1971 (44 games) and 1972 (60); Gene Clines took over in 1973 (55); Rennie Stennett did the job in 1974 (125) and 1975 (118); and Frank Taveras occupied the number-one slot in 1976 (105), 1977 (88), and 1978 (157).

In 1979, the Bucs then settled on Omar Moreno, a base-stealing outfielder, to set their offensive table. He held that position through the 1982 campaign. During his Pittsburgh tenure, Moreno copped two stolen base titles and led off 597 games. He compiled a .255 batting average and a .315 on base percentage — again, figures that certainly didn't erase the honored memory of Little Poison.

Marvell Wynne took over the principal leadoff duties for Pittsburgh in 1983 and 1984. And Joe Orsulak served as the primary table setter in 1985.

1986-1994
Perhaps the Best at the Top;
But Too Good to be There

As specified nowadays, the ideal leadoff batter is an "igniter"; a "make it happen" player — a batter who can get on base with hits and walks; advance into scoring position with a stolen base; and, if needed, blast the ball out of the park with regularity. Even Little Poison didn't possess all those attributes. But Barry Bonds does (certainly now). And he was the Pirate principal leadoff batter for four years beginning in 1986. During that stretch (427 first-up games), he assembled a batting average of only .256 and an on base percentage of just .347 — but he also walloped 84 homers and swiped 117 bases. Of course, during his next three years with Pittsburgh, Bonds blossomed. He greatly improved his batting and on base percentage without sacrificing power or base stealing prowess. By that point, he was utilized in the leadoff slot only infrequently (just 13 games) — he was simply too good to be there.

Instead, the Pirates relied on Wally Backman in 1990; Orlando Merced in 1991; and Gary Redus in 1992. Although none could have been called prototypical leadoff men, the Pirates won three straight division titles. And for the last two seasons, Pittsburgh has depended on Carlos — Carlos Garcia — to ignite the offense. While it's still early in the second baseman's career, he has demonstrated that he can pop the ball into the seats. Maybe in time, he'll be mentioned in the same breath with Little Poison.

Concluding Remarks

The top five number-one batters for the Pittsburgh Pirates during the 1920-1994 period were Lloyd Waner, with 1147 leadoff games; Bill Virdon, 634; Omar Moreno, 597; Matty Alou, 499; and Barry Bonds, 440.

Finally, it is interesting to note that some other Pirates with illustrious diamond credentials also occupied the leadoff slot, at least for one game during the "live ball" era: Hall of Famers Pie Traynor, 2 games; Kiki Cuyler, 2; Paul Waner, 101; Arky Vaughan, 1; Freddy Lindstrom, 19; and slugger Willie Stargell, 2.

A Lot of History at Three Rivers Stadium

Think they've been playing baseball here just since 1970? Think again.

By Dan Bonk

EVER SINCE THE NORTH SIDE was selected as the site of Pittsburgh's present municipally-financed, multi-purpose stadium, writers and historians have reminded us of a peculiar irony. Three Rivers Stadium, which in 1970 replaced Forbes Field, is built near the site of Exposition Park, the Pirate home before they moved to Forbes in 1909.

It is interesting that the exact location of the old ballpark is never mentioned and for that matter, hasn't been known since the old wooden ballpark was demolished in the early 1920s. But Exposition Park was the site of one of the most significant historical sporting events ever to occur in western Pennsylvania. In October 1903, Games 4,5,6 and 7 of the first modern World Series were played there. The Pirates lost that best-of-nine World Series in eight games to the Boston Pilgrims (their socks were not yet red) in what was to become the fall classic.

The World Series returned to Pittsburgh in Forbes Field's inaugural season of 1909. Forbes Field was hailed for its beauty, grandeur, and modern amenities when it opened for business in 1909. Many felt sadness and loss the day it closed. Its remnants in Oakland have become the focus of many baseball fan pilgrimages. Exposition Park, in contrast, slipped into the local consciousness without fanfare and left without a tear.

Exposition Park got its name from the Allegheny Exposition which occupied the shoreline north of Pittsburgh, (in what was then Allegheny City), for eight years beginning in 1875. The Exposition was constructed by the Tradesmen's Industrial Institute which was chartered to promote "a permanent exposition of the arts, sciences and industries of Western Pennsylvania." It consisted of a large exhibit hall and grounds which included an oval track for horse and bicycle racing.

In the summer of 1882, Pittsburgh's first major league baseball team, the American Association Alleghenies (what else would you call a Pittsburgh team that played its games in Allegheny City?) began playing their first season on a field laid out inside the race track oval at the Allegheny Exposition. In the fall of 1883, the Exposition buildings were destroyed by fire, leaving only the racetrack and horse stables. Major league baseball, as played by the Alleghenies and later by Pittsburgh's National League franchise, abandoned the Exposition grounds after the fire and played their games up the street at Recreation Park, which was located several blocks to the north.

In 1890, growing tension between professional ballplayers and ball club owners resulted in the formation of the Brotherhood League, a sort of 19th-century employee-owned enterprise. The Pittsburgh franchise, known as the Burghers, played in a new ballpark built on property leased at the old Exposition grounds.

The facility consisted primarily of a two-tiered, covered wooden grandstand with bench seats at the corner of South Avenue and School Street facing the Allegheny River and the Point. It was called Exposition Park so that the local populace, who fondly remembered the old Allegheny Exposition, would immediately know where it was. The outfield fence was located roughly 250 feet from the bank of

hard times in the 1890s due, in part, to the generally poor teams that Pittsburgh fielded.

The fortunes of the franchise changed dramatically in 1900 with the arrival of a new club president, Barney Dreyfuss. Dreyfuss was fiercely competitive and equally shrewd. He believed that baseball was a growth business and that Pittsburgh was a town where it could flourish. Thanks measurably to the presence of Honus Wagner, a local kid from Carnegie who would rapidly become baseball's biggest attraction in the first decade of the 20th century, the crowds flocked to Exposition Park. The

"The Point" in Pittsburgh, around 1905, showing Exposition Park in the upper left.

the Allegheny River. The Brotherhood League was out of business after just one season.

After the 1890 season, the Pittsburgh Nationals signed two unprotected players from the competing American Association and were branded forever as "Pirates." The new moniker was welcomed by franchise President J. Palmer O'Neill as he moved his team to one-year-old Exposition Park. The Pirates played their first game there on April 22, 1891, losing 7-6 to a Chicago team led by the legendary Cap Anson. Financially, the ball club fell upon

Pirates regularly played before crowds of 10,000 or more fans and soon became one of the most profitable franchises in the National League. This success did not go unnoticed. By the end of the 1902 season, the upstart American League was considering adding a Pittsburgh franchise to compete with the Pirates and was known to be seeking a site on which to build a new ballpark.

Dreyfuss, attempting to keep competition out of the Pittsburgh market, played a major role in the landmark 1903 peace agreement between the National and American Leagues. The savvy Dreyfuss made certain that the agreement included a provision that the American League would not enter Pittsburgh. By August 1903, it was evident that the Pirates would repeat as National League champions for the third straight season. In an effort to cement the still-tenuous peace, Dreyfuss and Boston owner Henry Killilea arranged a postseason series to determine a World Championship. Both leagues could clearly see that great interest and publicity could be generated among fans and media by such an event.

The World Series opened in Boston and when it returned to Pittsburgh, thousands of Pirate fans flocked to Exposition Park where the price of a seat was 50 cents. Local newspapers reported how hundreds of fans viewed the game for free, perched on top of Monument Hill just north of the park or across the river along Grandview Avenue atop Mt. Washington. (It is difficult to say how well the latter group of free-riders could have enjoyed the game, being well over a quarter-mile away.)

Although the World Series never again came to Exposition Park, its history book was not yet closed. Early in the 1909 season, newly elected President William Howard Taft attended a Pirate-Cub game at Exposition Park. Taft's favorite player was Honus Wagner, but his loyalties were compromised; Taft's brother was a part owner of the Cubs. Taft returned to Pittsburgh in 1910 and attended a game at Forbes Field. He remains the only U.S. President to watch the Pirates in Pittsburgh while in office.

The Pirates played their last game at Exposition Park on June 29, 1909, beating the Chicago Cubs, 8-1. Even without the Pirates, the ballpark was in demand and continued to flourish. From 1912 through 1915, would-be challengers to the National League, the United States League and the Federal League, fielded

teams at Exposition Park. However, by then the affections of Pittsburghers were firmly with the Pirates and the venue of choice was clearly Forbes Field, the finest ballpark in the country. Neither league lasted more than two seasons.

Utilization of Exposition Park diminished rapidly after 1915. Local high schools played baseball and football there as did various semipro and sandlot teams. On occasion, the Pitt Panther varsity and freshman football teams would play there rather than at Forbes Field when their schedules conflicted with the Pirates.

In the early 1920s, Exposition Park succumbed to the needs of its leaseholder, the Baltimore and Ohio Railroad. Rail lines and other support structures were built over the playing field. By 1925, the site was indistinguishable from the surrounding railroad yard. In 1968, construction of Three Rivers Stadium commenced and the same railroad yard was turned back into a ball yard.

Thanks to a group of local volunteers from the Pittsburgh Chapter of SABR the location of home plate at Exposition Park has been found. It is situated in a parking stall in Stadium Lot #4, between Gates B and C and the Fort Duquesne Bridge. A spray-painted home plate now marks the spot as the Pirates and the City of Pittsburgh consider a more appropriate and permanent means of identification. Fans of baseball and history can stand at the plate and conjure up images of the famous Americans who stood there long ago. Honus Wagner, Cap Anson, Cy Young, John McGraw, Connie Mack, Nap Lajoie, Christy Mathewson and Charlie Comiskey were there, as were Tinker, Evers and Chance of the famous baseball poem.

In other words, if you look carefully, you can find a lot of history in a parking stall at Three Rivers Stadium.

The Worst Moments in Pirate Baseball History

Some teams suffer for decades; the Bucs do it by minutes

By Paul Adomites

As MOST CLUBS THAT HAVE BEEN around for a hundred years or more, the Pirates have their share of historical glory and adventure. Interestingly (and unlike many other long-lived teams), the Pirates have usually been in contention or in the middle of the pack (just one more solid lefty away, we have said) for most seasons of their history. They have not had an extended run of futility, with the exception of the 1949-57 era, which was jam-packed with laughs, at least. When the Bucs **were** bad, they were horrid in legendary fashion.

The bad times for the Pirates seem to happen in terrible **moments**; both on and off the field. They let themselves down with dreadful mistakes; they were victimized by heroic efforts by opponents who ranged from Hall of Famers to absolute nobodies; a corporation removed one of their most beloved figures in a snit; one of their greatest stars was taken from them while on a mission of mercy.

Here then is a brief listing of those miserable moments in the history of the Pittsburgh major league baseball franchise. Let the pains begin.

The Big Serb and the 1927 World Series

The story is a pleasing incident in baseball mythology, apparently created by Ford Frick, later to become baseball commissioner, but at the time a sportswriter for one of the New York dailies. As the tale goes, the Pirates watched the Yankees take batting practice before the Series' first game, and were "in awe" of the Yankee size and slugging capability. Properly abashed, the Bucs fell apart instantly under the crush of the Yank juggernaut and were swept in four games.

Well, it was a sweep, all right. But the other "facts" fall down under closer consideration. The Yanks may have been large, but the Pirates were no wimps. The Waners, Traynor, Glenn Wright and George Grantham were rugged dudes. No Pirate who was asked later remembered watching Yankee batting practice. Why should they? These were the same New Yorkers the Cards had taken out in the '26 Series.

In Game 1, two Pirate misplays gave the Yanks the second-inning runs they needed for a 5-4 win. No one homered. Game 2 was much the same. If not for a Pirate wild pitch and hit batter in the eighth inning, the final score would have been 3-2. Again, no home runs. Where was this legendary Yankee power? Hadn't this team just set the record for homers in a season?

It appeared only in Game 3. Ruth slugged a three-run shot in the last of the eighth to help the Yanks to an 8-1 win.

The final game was tight from the beginning. Both teams scored in the first. New York added a pair on a Ruth homer in the fifth, but the Buccos fought back. The Yanks, who had made just one error in the Series' first three games, made consecutive bobbles to open the top of the seventh. The Pirates scored twice to tie things up at 3. John Miljus, known affectionately as "The Big Serb," got Ruth to ground into a double play in the last of the seventh, and stranded two Yank runners in the last of the eighth.

In the ninth he lost it. After walking Combs and seeing Koenig beat out a bunt, The Big Serb uncorked a wild pitch with Babe Ruth at bat. Manager Donie Bush ordered Ruth passed to load the bases. Miljus then came close to becoming a World Series immortal. He struck out both Lou Gehrig and Bob Meusel (with the bases loaded and nobody out!) But the "sailor" he tossed to Tony Lazzeri went over catcher Gooch's shoulder. Two wild pitches in the ninth inning of a close World Series game shut down the Pirates.

Things might have been different if the Pirates hadn't benched Kiki Cuyler during the Series for....well, that's another story.

Gabby Hartnett's 'Homer in the Gloaming' (and the Hurricane)

By September 1, 1938, the Pirates (who had barely sniffed first place since the 1927 Series disaster) were out in front of the Chicago Cubs by seven games. But as a hurricane swatted the Atlantic Coast, the red-hot Bucs were cooled off by having several series washed out. The Cubs made their move.

On September 20, the Pirate lead was half what it had been 19 days before, but Commissioner Landis still felt justified in permitting the Pittsburgh club to sell World Series tickets. Owner Bill Benswanger (son-in-law of Barney Dreyfuss, given the job because Dreyfuss's son Sammy had died in 1931) built a spectacular new press box atop Forbes Field for the upcoming event. But the rains kept coming, and the Buccos stumbled. By the time

they reached Chicago on September 27 for a three-game series, the Cubs were just 1-1/2 games behind.

Dizzy Dean, whom the Cubs had acquired from the Cardinals for $185,000 and three players in April, started the first game. Dean's arm was dead, but his savvy wasn't. He stopped the Pirates on seven hits, winning 2-1. It was only his seventh win of the season, but he had also lost just once.

September 28 was a gloomy day in Chicago. Johnny Rizzo helped the Pirates to an early 3-1 lead, but with the score tied at 3 in the seventh and two men on, Johnny slapped into a double play (the Pirates claimed Vance Page had balked on the pitch.) The Bucs pushed over two more runs in the eighth, but the Cubs replied with a pair in their half. It could have been more, but pinch runner Joe Marty was thrown out at home, and Pirate relief ace Mace Brown (the first reliever to be called "the fireman") got Frank Demaree to ground into a snappy twin killing.

Before the ninth inning began, the umpires met at home plate to decide whether there was enough light to continue playing. "One more inning," was their decision. The Pirates didn't score in their half, and Brown easily retired the first two batters in the Cubs ninth.

Then Hartnett came to the plate. He swung and missed Brown's first curveball. Brown remembered thinking Hartnett "looked like a schoolboy," and decided to stick with his breaking pitch. Hartnett fouled the next one off. Oh-and-two. Then Brown threw another curve, but right where Hartnett wanted it and he poked it into the leftfield bleachers. It was so dark by that time that most observers never saw where it went.

The demoralized Pirates were crushed the next day 10-1 and won just one more game of the season's final four. The Pirates finished two games back, but ended the year with four unplayed games: two each with cellar-dwellers Brooklyn and Philadelphia.

1972 — Bob Moose does a Serbian impression

Events in baseball history echo off each other like balls rattling around the corners in Ebbets or Forbes. Bob Moose and John Miljus were both Pittsburghers pitching for their home town team. Both would die in 1976. And in the ninth inning of the final National League Championship Series of 1972, Moose would echo Miljus by throwing a wild pitch that kept the Pirates from playing for the World Championship.

The 1972 Pirates might have been a better team than the 1971 World Champion edition. Several members of both teams thought so. While the 1971 Pirates had more power, the 1972 pitching staff was vastly superior. The team's ERA was half a run better; all four starters flirted with the 3.00 mark. Reliever Dave Giusti, aided by the addition of Ramon Hernandez, slashed his own ERA by a full run.

But the Bucs were going up against a young new challenger to the NL throne, a team that would earn a place as one of the greatest of all time, and become known as "The Big Red Machine."

Each team won two of the first four games. Steve Blass was strong in Game 1, Bob Moose pitched to five batters in Game 2 and didn't get anyone out as the Reds scored four times. The Pirates came back from a 2-0 Red lead in Game 3 to win, but were stopped cold by Don Gullett on two hits (both by Roberto Clemente) in Game 4.

October 11, 1972 marked the first time that the 1969-instituted League Championship Series had gone to a full five games. (Detroit and Oakland would do the same the next day.) The Pirates took a 3-2 lead into the bottom of the ninth, and Manager Bill Virdon brought in top reliever Dave Giusti to shut down the Red righthanded power. In Pittsburgh we were busy discussing who we would rather face in the Series, Oakland or Detroit. But Giusti threw a slider too high to Johnny Bench, and the Red catcher hit it over the rightfield fence to tie the game. Giusti was touched for consecutive singles and Virdon turned to Moose.

A long fly to right moved pinch runner George Foster to third. Darrel Chaney popped up. Moose's first pitch to Hal McRae was a strike. Then he threw a ball. The third pitch skipped away from Manny Sanguillen and the Reds had won.

The death of Roberto

Less than three months after the Moose wild pitch, Pittsburgh baseball fans had to endure another horrifying moment when our noble superstar, Roberto Clemente, died in a plane crash while trying to deliver supplies to Nicaraguan earthquake victims. Clemente was on the plane because he suspected some of the supplies he had raised money for were being commandeered by less-than-honorable men. The plane was probably overloaded and in poor flying condition; the pilots were not known for their airworthiness.

The shock struck the city like a meteor. Clemente had turned 38 years old in August, but he had nearly led the Pirates to another World Series. He looked much more like a brash 30-year-old than a tiring oldster. The disbelief turned into a wash of grief; hundreds of people, desperate to express their feelings for the proud and regal Clemente, wrote letters, poems and songs about him and sent them to the Pirate offices. The team flew to Puerto Rico but one player didn't join them for the funeral service. Manny Sanguillen, Clemente's best friend on the team, was in the ocean near where the plane went down, scuba diving in a futile attempt to locate his **amigo**.

Clemente had come to racially backward Pittsburgh in 1955, a black man barely able to speak English, and with sheer determination and pride became one of the world's best ballplayers. At the same time his devotion to serving others with hands-on charitable work and dedication made him truly beloved here. The remarkable statue of him now proudly posed at Gate A at Three Rivers Stadium is a small memento to the place he held in the hearts of Pittsburgh.

They fired the Gunner!

For more than 25 years, Bob Prince was the voice of the Pirates. His brash style, unabashed rooting and lovable catch phrases ("Call a **doc**-tor!") were not only Pittsburgh staples of summer, but known across the country because of radio station KDKA's 50,000-watt clear channel signal. Prince was able to stir up Pittsburgh fandom to attend games even when the team wasn't of championship caliber. He was as much a Pittsburgh institution as anyone had ever been.

But by the middle 1970s, things were changing in baseball. The fan most desired by management wasn't the typical beer-drinking, belly-scratching laborer who could afford a dozen games a year. Corporate America was sliding its tentacles around baseball. And not surprisingly, Bob Prince and corporate America were oil and water.

The Westinghouse Broadcasting Company, owner of KDKA and a division of Westinghouse Electric Corporation, enjoyed treating customers to games at Three Rivers, and inviting them into the broadcast booth to see Prince work. The corporate bigwigs were often out for a good time more than they were out to see a ballgame, and Prince wasn't afraid to scold them. Westinghouse didn't feel that Prince was behaving like a good corporate citizen, and dropped him from the broadcasts shortly after in the Pirate LCs loss to Cincy in 1975.

In some ways Pittsburgh baseball never recovered. With the Prince boosterish qualities gone, replaced by the barely-awake drone of Milo Hamilton, the team's attendance plummeted, even during championship seasons. The Pittsburgh corporation had managed to move baseball away from the forefront of the city's consciousness. (Ironically it would be a group of local corporations, among them Westinghouse, that would rescue the team and keep it in town ten years later.)

They brought Bob Prince back in the middle of the ineffably miserable 1985 season. They had already tried to boost sagging interest by rehiring legend Willie Stargell as first-base coach. Prince was hired from a sickbed to return to the broadcast booth. Despite a ravaged voice and frail constitution, what a comeback "the Gunner" made: the first inning he broadcast was in a game against the Dodgers. The usually surehanded men from Los Angeles went haywire and handed the Bucs nine runs.

In the next inning, Jason Thompson headed to the plate, and "The Gunner" said, "Jason, old boy, put one out of here now and we'll have a little of everything." Thompson promptly skied a homer into the right field seats, which prompted Prince to say to his booth partner: "If this keeps up, you can carry me out of here on my shield." But that would be the last inning Prince ever broadcast for the Pirates. Five weeks later he was dead.

Cabrera

The name simultaneously evokes a carbine, the line drive shot through the left side of the Pirate infield, and a sombrero, the hat Barry Bonds' bat must have worn during its postseason siestas. The Pirates had been toppled during the league championship series of 1990 because their pitching was worn so thin that ancient reliever Ted Power had to start the final game, and thumped in the 1991 LCS by hot Brave starters who threw shutouts.

The 1992 Series was much more evenly matched, as the Pirates called on the Magic of Sir Wakefield of Knuckledom, and he responded nobly, with two shutouts. Game 7 saw the Bucs take a 2-0 lead into the last of the ninth, only to have, in order: (and I'm not making this up) 1) Their best starter, Drabek, fall victim to a bad play by their best infielder, Lind; 2) their best reliever, Belinda, stymied by a bad call by the home plate ump; and 3) their best player, Bonds, unable to make a decent throw home to nail the gimpy-legged former Pirate Sid Bream (never in the Coleman class to begin with.)

And to play what-if for just another second, had the usually strong-armed Bonds

A determined Doug Drabek.

cut down Bream, the Bucs were sitting in the Pittsburgh equivlent of the catbird seat. Jim Leyland had outmanaged Bobby Cox so completely that the Brave skipper would have been forced to start the tenth inning with a pitcher in the outfield. With that unlikely combination of Pirate maledicta all taking place in the space of minutes, the Braves went to the World Series, as you recall.

God, it hurt.

It has become fashionable to deconstruct the events of that evening as concrete expression of the eternal myth of how money or the lack of it ruins ball clubs. Bream, despite being a longtime Pittsburgh fan favorite, had left (even though he said he wouldn't) for bigger dollars. Bobby Bonilla, paragon of tact and ambassador of love, had jumped, too. Bonds and Drabek were on their way out. Bonds even spent an Atlanta afternoon during the LCS shopping for real estate in case the Braves made him an offer worthy of his talents. (Was he fantasizing about a particularly lovely chalet in Marietta when Cabrera hit the ball to him?) And some have berated Leyland for not calling to the heavens for one more dose of Wakefield.

The facts are soggier. But the truth is, the Braves did it when the Pirates didn't. That's okay. Baseball is a delightful haven of what-iffery, but it is also delightful in its crystal clarity. Lavalliere reaches for the throw up the first-base line, hoping his arms could suddenly become six inches longer. Bream slides under the tag, Braves win, Pirates lose. Atlanta goes to the World Series and the Pirate mini-dynasty of the 1990s disappears in a puff of perhaps.

EPILOGUE: Off the field, at least, the tradition of horrible Pirate moments may have changed its spots. There was the abysmal 1985 season, during which the team was for sale but no one who wanted to keep it in town could afford it, and many members of the team spent their spare time testifying in a Pittsburgh drug trial. With the team up for sale again nine years later, Pittsburgh fans have had to continue another extended ordeal of agony as corporate ego and baseball's precarious financial structure (not to mention the evil strike) dragged out interminably.